**New Directions for
Teaching and Learning**

Marilla D. Svinicki
EDITOR-IN-CHIEF

R. Eugene Rice
CONSULTING EDITOR

Decoding the Disciplines: Helping Students Learn Disciplinary Ways of Thinking

David Pace
Joan Middendorf
EDITORS

Number 98 • Summer 2004
Jossey-Bass
San Francisco

DECODING THE DISCIPLINES: HELPING STUDENTS LEARN DISCIPLINARY WAYS OF
THINKING
David Pace, Joan Middendorf (eds.)
New Directions for Teaching and Learning, no. 98
Marilla D. Svinicki, Editor-in-Chief
R. Eugene Rice, Consulting Editor

Microfilm copies of issues and articles are available in 16mm and 35mm,
as well as microfiche in 105mm, through University Microfilms Inc., 300
North Zeeb Road, Ann Arbor, Michigan 48106-1346.

NEW DIRECTIONS FOR TEACHING AND LEARNING (ISSN 0271-0633, electronic
ISSN 1536-0768) is part of The Jossey-Bass Higher and Adult Education
Series and is published quarterly by Wiley Subscription Services, Inc., A
Wiley Company, at Jossey-Bass, 989 Market Street, San Francisco, Cali-
fornia 94103-1741. Periodicals postage paid at San Francisco, California,
and at additional mailing offices. POSTMASTER: Send address changes to
New Directions for Teaching and Learning, Jossey-Bass, 989 Market Street,
San Francisco, California 94103-1741.

New Directions for Teaching and Learning is indexed in College Student
Personnel Abstracts, Contents Pages in Education, and Current Index to
Journals in Education (ERIC).

SUBSCRIPTIONS cost $80 for individuals and $170 for institutions, agencies,
and libraries. Prices subject to change. See order form at end of book.

EDITORIAL CORRESPONDENCE should be sent to the editor-in-chief, Marilla
D. Svinicki, The Center for Teaching Effectiveness, University of Texas at
Austin, Main Building 2200, Austin, TX 78712-1111.

www.josseybass.com

CONTENTS

About This Publication. Since 1980, *New Directions for Teaching and Learning (NDTL)* has brought a unique blend of theory, research, and practice to leaders in postsecondary education. *NDTL* sourcebooks strive not only for solid substance but also for timeliness, compactness, and accessibility.

The series has four goals: to inform readers about current and future directions in teaching and learning in postsecondary education, to illuminate the context that shapes these new directions, to illustrate these new directions through examples from real settings, and to propose ways in which these new directions can be incorporated into still other settings.

This publication reflects the view that teaching deserves respect as a high form of scholarship. We believe that significant scholarship is conducted not only by researchers who report results of empirical investigations but also by practitioners who share disciplined reflections about teaching. Contributors to *NDTL* approach questions of teaching and learning as seriously as they approach substantive questions in their own disciplines, and they deal not only with pedagogical issues but also with the intellectual and social context in which these issues arise. Authors deal on the one hand with theory and research and on the other with practice, and they translate from research and theory to practice and back again.

About This Volume. Research in psychology has shown that there are indeed disciplinary differences in the way we think about our subjects. Our position as experts in our fields sometimes blinds us to the fact that students have been trained to think differently. An important first step in socializing students into our discipline is to help them understand how we think. This issue reports the results of an institution-wide project at Indiana University in which faculty used a common model to help uncover for the students the uncommon thinking strategies inherent in each discipline.

Marilla D. Svinicki
Editor-in-Chief

MARILLA D. SVINICKI *is director of the Center for Teaching Effectiveness at the University of Texas at Austin.*

1

Using the Decoding the Disciplines model, faculty who are deeply ingrained in their disciplinary research answer a series of questions to understand how students think and learn in their field. The cross-disciplinary nature of the process clarifies the thinking for each discipline.

Decoding the Disciplines: A Model for Helping Students Learn Disciplinary Ways of Thinking

Joan Middendorf, David Pace

In the last twenty years, the call for faculty members to focus on critical thinking has led to a laudable effort on the part of faculty members and teaching support professionals to move the focus of courses to the higher levels of Bloom's (1956) classification of learning behaviors. But efforts to help students learn at the levels of analysis, synthesis, and evaluation may be impeded by a mismatch between the kinds of thinking actually required in specific classes and generic formulas for encouraging higher-order thinking. In fact, the notion of a unified "critical thinking" runs counter to an important strand in current thinking about teaching that stresses the disciplinary nature of knowledge.

Critical Thinking and the Disciplines

In the last twenty years, a number of major researchers have stressed the importance of shaping instruction to match the specific conditions of each academic field. In his 1986 inaugural address as president of the American Educational Research Association, Lee Shulman argued that whereas teacher training had been dominated by a focus on mastering disciplinary content

We want to thank Ray Smith, Jennifer Robinson, the fellows of the Indiana University Faculty Learning Community, the staff of Instructional Support Services, the Dean of Faculties Office, and the Lilly foundation for the generous support that made this project possible.

in the nineteenth century and on assimilating generic educational theory in the first three quarters of the twentieth century, attention should be henceforth expanded to the study of learning in the particular contexts created by specific disciplines (Shulman, 1987). In the same period, other scholars were developing the notion of "cognitive apprenticeship" in which the process of learning an academic discipline was compared with learning to function in a foreign culture (Brown, Collins, and Duguid, 1989). And in the 1990s, the importance of the differences among disciplines was made even clearer by Tobias, who observed the difficulties that even intelligent and highly trained instructors and graduate students faced when they were transplanted into undergraduate courses far removed from their own specialties (Tobias, 1992–1993).

Two different but important approaches have made progress in understanding the way knowledge is structured and how experts think in specific disciplines. Donald (2002) represents higher-order thinking in several disciplines to show how faculty and students perceive the learning process, while the Committee on Developments in the Science of Learning (Bransford, Brown, and Cocking, 2000) links the scientific study of thinking and learning to classroom practices. Even though their approaches differ, both reach the conclusion that disciplines need to be more involved in the research on how people think and how students learn. Donald states, "There is a substantial convergence in the need for deeper understanding of the disciplines. The continuing challenge is how to draw on the expertise of scholars to improve post-secondary education" (2002, p. 299). Thus, we have only begun to understand what kind of thinking goes on in different disciplines, nor do we know the similarities and differences across the disciplines.

This concern with the disciplinary nature of learning has been one of the primary motivations for the development of a scholarship of teaching and learning in which faculty from across universities make contributions to pedagogical literature (Hutchings and Shulman, 1999; Huber and Morreale, 2002). Many of the essays in this volume are examples of this kind of extension of the responsibility for thinking and writing about teaching and learning.

The contributors in this volume are from fields as diverse as creative writing, marketing, and genetics. They have a deep understanding of the content of their disciplines, and now they want to understand how students learn this content. Their chapters show faculty in the disciplines doing this kind of work and provide what we have named "Decoding the Disciplines," a process for getting them deeply into the specifics of thinking and learning in their disciplines.

But these efforts did not begin as an endeavor to stimulate such scholarship. Instead, they emerged from an attempt to bridge the gap between the marvelous strategies for increasing learning that have emerged from educational research in the past several decades and the concrete experiences

Figure 1.1. Decoding the Disciplines: Seven Steps to Overcome Obstacles to Learning

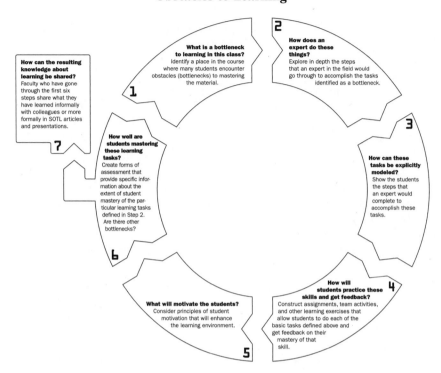

of faculty trying to help students master specific material in particular disciplines.

The story of how the Decoding the Disciplines model is used in the Indiana University Faculty Learning Community (IUFLC) will be left until Chapter Ten. For now, suffice to say that each year ten to twelve faculty from across the disciplines participate in a two-week seminar in which they practice new teaching strategies and serve as students for each other. The IUFLC arose from a strong realization that the mental operations required of undergraduates differ enormously from discipline to discipline, that these ways of thinking are rarely presented to students explicitly, that students generally lack an opportunity to practice and receive feedback on particular skills in isolation from others, and that there is rarely a systematic assessment of the extent to which students have mastered each of the ways of thinking that are essential to particular disciplines. The result of ten iterations of this FLC was a seven-step framework (see Figure 1.1) within which teachers can develop strategies for introducing students to the culture of thinking in a specific discipline and, in the process, level the playing field for those students who do not come to college "preeducated."

There is nothing mechanical or deterministic about these steps. Rather, they serve as a series of questions that instructors can ask themselves as they work on responding to the specific challenges posed by learning in their disciplines. This process emerged from a shared effort involving more than fifty faculty members who have used this general model to produce their own strategies for helping their students overcome bottlenecks to learning in their classes. This approach does not stand in opposition to other, preexisting strategies for increasing learning. The structure within which the authors in this volume have worked has, in fact, made it easier to make effective use of such methods as active, collaborative, and inquiry-based instruction. The systematic identification of what students have difficulty learning and what they should know how to do makes the design of methods for practice and effective assessments relatively straightforward. But the application of this approach by the IUFLC fellows has produced some remarkable solutions to learning challenges in a wide range of disciplines, and we hope that process described here can be adopted and adapted by other institutions.

The remainder of this chapter serves as an introduction to the Decoding the Disciplines model that has helped the contributors of this volume and faculty in other programs at this and other universities become more effective teachers and advocates for student learning. We believe that this work will respond to two central questions in contemporary pedagogy: First, how is the nature of disciplines to be brought into the discussion of teaching and learning? Decoding the Disciplines places disciplines at the center of the discussions of teaching, and paradoxically, the cross-disciplinary nature of the work clarifies thinking in the disciplines themselves. As contributors Durisen and Pilachowski conclude in Chapter Four, "Interactions with faculty in different disciplines clarified the role of discipline-specific thinking in teaching and learning and helped us to recognize the learning strategies that our students bring to their study of astronomy."

Second, this work may also provide a means of answering a second crucial question: How can faculty in all disciplines be encouraged to become involved in the scholarship of teaching and learning? Many of the essays in this volume serve as evidence that the Decoding the Disciplines model can give faculty who have never thought of publishing about teaching the tools they need to conduct such inquiry. It focuses their attention on crucial difficulties students have in learning their disciplines, gives them a framework within which to respond to these challenges, and provides them with models with which to assess evidence of student learning.

Step 1. What Is a Bottleneck to Learning in This Class?

Decoding the Disciplines begins with a simple task: identifying bottlenecks—that is, points in a course where the learning of a significant number of students is interrupted (Anderson, 1996). Virtually anyone who has set foot in a classroom can identify some area in which learning has not occurred in ways that the instructor wished it to. Like many of these steps in this process, this question seems so obvious that it is surprising in retrospect how often it is omitted. But in practice, many efforts to reshape classes begin with questions such as, how can I make use of this new technique? Or, how can I increase my students' critical thinking? Such questions are often too broad to provide a clear focal point for designing more effective strategies. They sometimes draw attention to parts of the course that are not in great need of reform, and they generally focus the process on the means (teaching) rather than the end (student learning).

In the FLC seminars, there is a tactical advantage to beginning with the bottlenecks defined by the fellows because this makes their instructional concerns central to the process. This approach also focuses the process at the points where change is most needed, and it tends to narrow the work to a "chunk size" that can be dealt with more readily. Because faculty can often identify numerous places where there seem to be obstacles to learning, it is important to prioritize those that most seriously interfere with the central learning in a course. The nature of these obstacles may vary considerably, with some involving both cognitive and affective elements and others more narrowly intellectual.

Step 2. How Does an Expert Do These Things?

The second step in this process is for faculty to reconstruct the steps that they themselves do when solving similar problems. This is generally the most intellectually demanding of all the steps in the Decoding the Disciplines approach. The research of Donald (2002), Tobias (1992–1993), Wineberg (2001), and Bransford, Brown, and Cocking (2000) has demonstrated how varied the thinking is in different disciplines, and the uniqueness of particular ways of posing and solving problems is often invisible to professionals in the field. This step is difficult because it requires metacognition: faculty have to dissect their own innate thinking. Faculty generally chose to go into fields where they were successful at that kind of thinking and have been working within that particular disciplinary framework for years. Therefore, they may have leaped almost automatically over obstacles that can prove daunting for novices.

Instructors in every discipline can begin this process of exploring its specific ways of operating by working to distance themselves from all that is natural and automatic to members of their field. We facilitate this process in the IUFLC by having the fellows from different disciplines work together so that they will be less likely to skip over steps that are "intuitively obvious." Taking inspiration from the experiments of Tobias, we also sent the fellows into classes that were as far removed from their own specialty as possible. For example, the historians attended a genetics class, the geneticists attended a philosophy of art class, and the humanities professors attended finite math courses, all with instructions to take notes as if they were to be examined on the material.

But the most intense intervention involved a ninety-minute interview in which each fellow had to explain in precise detail just what an expert would do if faced with one of the tasks that students had difficulty completing successfully. Typically, the instructor would provide an initial response that contained unexplained terms and undefined processes that seemed too obvious to be consciously recalled. The task of the interviewers was to repeatedly probe beneath the surface, asking questions such as, "Just how are the students supposed to do that?" or, "What does that instruction assume that students are able to do?" In the process they go from a vaguely worded idea such as "critical thinking" to a more detailed analysis of the kinds of thinking their students need to master. For example, a creative writing professor realized he had to model the process of choosing descriptive images and words. And a molecular biology professor realized he had to teach students to visualize complex molecular structures as dynamic three-dimensional cartoons, just as he did. During the interview, fellows often experience an "aha" moment. The interviews give them a preview of how deeply they will examine their students' thinking.

These interviews can be duplicated in almost any educational institution by having instructors in different fields explain to each other how an expert would overcome an obstacle that seems daunting to many of their students. Anyone who attempts this will have to remember to remain focused on what an expert does and not on the content of the lesson or the steps that might be taken to teach students this skill. And it will generally be necessary to probe many levels beneath the surface because the initial response will almost certainly pass over steps that are so obvious to the expert that they are not even noticed.

Step 3. How Can These Tasks Be Explicitly Modeled?

The next step is to devise ways to demonstrate to students the steps that come naturally to the expert. There will generally be a need to set priorities and to determine which operations are most essential and thus most important to model. In some cases, this may entail some systematic assessment of the levels of mastery of these operations that typically exist among the students at the beginning of the course. But we strongly encourage anyone using this method to devote some time to deciding which of these basic skills do or do not have be modeled; this will probably determine which members of the class will be included in the learning process, and that decision has important ethical and political dimensions.

Once one has decided which basic operations should be modeled, it is then time to devise demonstrations that will help students to begin to understand what this kind of thinking entails. Like the second stage of the Decoding the Disciplines model, this often requires serious intellectual labor, and it can be one of the most exhilarating parts of the process. In most cases, a good deal of redundancy will need to be built into the process and operations presented in several ways. Chapters Two and Five in this volume provide strong examples of faculty modeling their thinking. In addition to faculty demonstrating the kind of thinking they want students to do, in some cases (Chapters Three, Five, and Seven), faculty have to walk the students through an exercise to build bit by bit the mental model that faculty use. This is still part of the modeling step; it is not to be confused with the practice exercises of step 4.

It is important to remember both that complex ways of thinking are rarely assimilated in a single presentation and that different groups of students internalize such learning in different modalities (for example, visually, orally, and kinesthetically). Thus, it is often desirable to repeat the modeling on several occasions (MacKinnon, 2003) and in several different media (for example, in a classroom presentation and a class Web site). Finally, it is wise strategically to build modeling exercises around content that is particularly essential to the course so that the time devoted to modeling serves other purposes for the course as well.

Step 4. How Will Students Practice These Skills and Get Feedback?

Whereas in step 3 the instructor demonstrates the intellectual skill that the students need to learn, the focus in step 4 is to have the students practice the task and gauge the proficiency of their attempts. Decoding the Disciplines breaks down the basic operations required in a particular class and presents them systematically to students. But students can rarely move directly from hearing a complex set of operations described to internalizing the steps and then to applying them as part of a larger task some weeks later. Learning to think and work within the culture of a particular discipline is more complex than generally appears to be the case to professionals in the field, and students must be given a chance to perfect these skills and to receive feedback that clarifies where they are and are not succeeding. We need only imagine ourselves in a learning situation that is unfamiliar to us—a first lesson in knitting, a new computer program, or the grammar of a foreign language—to realize that simply hearing a lecture on a complex process is rarely sufficient to permit us to actually perform the task and to integrate it with dozens of other new procedures.

At this point, the marvelous new learning tools created over the past several decades can be integrated into the process. All the strategies associated with active, collaborative, and inquiry-based learning can be used to help students master the operations once they have been modeled, as seen in Chickering (1991), Yuretich (2004), Silberman (1996), Smith and MacGregor (1992), Michaelsen (1997), Wright (1994), and DiPasquale, Mason, and Kolkhorst (2003).

The process of defining and subdividing these operations, in fact, makes the application of such strategies particularly effective. Creating an exercise to allow students to actively perform some complex and ill-defined act of critical thinking is difficult, and it is not likely to provide students with clear feedback on their performance. If students do not succeed at a task that requires the integration of a half dozen discrete but undefined operations, they are not likely to be able to distinguish between skills they have mastered and those that must still be learned. By contrast, instructors who have gone through the first three steps of the Decoding the Disciplines process have already defined the focal point for such exercises, and they need only generate a framework within which these operations can be practiced one after another. Once a particular set of skills has been mastered by most of the class, the instructor can begin to generate more complex exercises that provide the occasion for synthesis and application. And throughout this process, the instructor can make strategic decisions about the subject matter used in these exercises to be sure that the time spent on these skills reinforces the most essential topics in the course.

Step 5. What Will Motivate the Students?

In the earlier stages of the development of this model, motivation was treated almost as an afterthought. But as we worked with successive generations of FLC fellows, it became increasingly clear that motivation was of sufficient importance to warrant its own position in the sequence of steps. If the students are not drawn actively into the modeling and the practice-and-feedback phases of the process, real learning is highly unlikely to occur.

Fortunately, the structure of this system lends itself to the application of the kinds of strategies supported by the literature on motivation (Svinicki, 1999; Perry, Menec, and Struthers, 1995). If, as the ancient Roman rhetorician Quintilian argued, "The job of the teacher is to arrange victories for the students," the Decoding the Disciplines process helps set the stage for a series of small but cumulative successes. Because large, complex tasks are divided into their constituent parts and each part is modeled and practiced, students are more apt to conceptualize their situation as one in which it is possible to learn and in which success or failure is seen in terms of their own effort, rather than luck.

It is not sufficient to assume that the structures of learning created by this process will automatically motivate students. Conscious effort needs to be dedicated to making the students partners in the learning process. The nature of this process allows an instructor to present himself or herself as an ally who has devoted considerable energy to creating a course in which success is possible and who really wants students to do well. Students often respond positively to instructors who are clearly dedicated to creating a level playing field on which students who have not been preeducated at elite institutions will have the same opportunity to succeed as those who have been more privileged.

It is, however, also important to avoid any sense that there is something remedial about this process. High expectations are an essential element in any meaningful strategy for increasing student motivation. The Decoding the Disciplines model substitutes a series of small, manageable steps for the giant leaps required in many traditional courses, but students should be expected to cover the same intellectual distance as they would in other courses. And there is a good chance that this approach will actually require students to work more.

Step 6. How Well Are Students Mastering These Learning Tasks?

In the past, faculty have often found themselves in a dilemma. On the one hand, the focus was on content learning that seemed to be relatively easy to assess but that did not reach the level of thinking that most faculty members desire to generate in their students. On the other was critical thinking, which dealt with an appropriate cognitive level but was generally perceived as impossible to assess (Cohen, 1987). In popular discussions, critical thinking often involves a number of different mental processes that are neither clearly defined nor adequately distinguished from one another. It is difficult to be certain when enough of these complex and often vague attributes are sufficiently in evidence to declare that the threshold of critical thinking has been reached.

The more precisely defined operations that are at the core of Decoding the Disciplines make assessment a different matter altogether. Because instructors have already broken bottlenecks down into the constituent parts that they want their students to learn, it is much easier to determine whether students have mastered them. Angelo and Cross's (1993) Classroom Assessment Techniques provide a good starting place for faculty to learn assessment methods, with simple and direct ways to determine whether students were able to perform specific disciplinary operations. Faculty have adapted these techniques or devised other ways to gauge student understanding. Often exercises that provide students with an opportunity to practice and receive feedback automatically provide the instructor with a good deal of information about what is and is not being learned. But as the essays that make up this volume amply demonstrate, the mastery of defined disciplinary operations can be assessed in a great variety of ways.

The assessments that emerge from this process are also more useful. It is easy to find out which of the basic operations are being mastered by most of the students and which need to be modeled or practiced more effectively or repeated several times during the course. Moreover, the skills being assessed are precisely those that the instructor has defined as most important for this particular class, an important consideration when more accountability is being demanded of higher education.

Step 7. How Can the Resulting Knowledge About Learning Be Shared?

This step of sharing initially arose out of the institutional concerns surrounding the IUFLC. The investment of resources that Indiana University was making in a relatively small number of instructors could be justified only if the ideas that the fellows developed in the program were shared with other faculty. Over time, however, we have come to recognize that this step is an integral part of the process. Those of us who employ collaborative strategies in our teaching often tell our students that they do not fully understand something until they have succeeded in explaining it to someone else. Our experiences in the IUFLC have convinced us that this is just as true for instructors. The process of sharing teaching goals and strategies forces us to make explicit elements that might otherwise have escaped our notice, to see possibilities that had previously escaped us, and to recognize inconsistencies or flawed logic. All of this can be cycled back into the process of course development to steadily increase learning in our classes.

The sharing of knowledge may occur in many forms. At one extreme is a simple conversation with colleagues; at the other, publication of one's findings in refereed journals and even large grants for building on one's work. And in between are such means of sharing as presentations of model lessons to other faculty, the exchange of course modules by instructors teaching similar courses as well as course portfolios.

But whatever the medium of sharing, the steps of the Decoding the Disciplines process make the interchange easier. The specificity of the focus, the clarity of the modeling, the ingenuity of the practice exercises, and the weight of the assessments all make it easier for instructors to learn from each others' experiments in the classroom. And, ironically, an approach that begins with an emphasis on the differences among disciplines can in the end provide a means to communicate across the chasms that separate academic fields.

In conclusion, it is important to stress that the Decoding the Disciplines approach should not be viewed as a narrow, prescriptive formula for all course development. The steps evolved as part of a group process of shared pedagogical exploration (see Chapter Ten). In other contexts, new steps may be necessary; some of ours may not be relevant; and the concrete strategies for defining, modeling, and providing practice may be completely different from those presented in this volume. This is only a tool, and it must therefore be adapted to the task at hand.

We have found that this approach has served to help many of the IUFLC fellows not only find new ways to enhance learning in their classes but also bring a new excitement to their teaching. The model serves to link teaching more closely with the kind of intellectual inquiry that drew the fellows toward being teachers in the first place, and it allows them to bring to teaching more of the skills that they have developed in their research. It also takes advantage of the differences in thinking among academic fields to decode each individual discipline. The energy that this process has engendered has carried the contributors to this volume beyond their individual disciplines into the scholarship of teaching and learning. We hope that the essays contained in this volume will convey this excitement to our readers.

References

Anderson, J. A. "Merging Teaching Effectiveness, Learning Outcomes, and Curricular Change with the Diverse Student Needs of the 21st Century." Paper presented at the 21st annual conference of the Professional and Organizational Development Network, Salt Lake City, Oct. 1996.

Angelo, T. A., and Cross, K. P. *Classroom Assessment Techniques: A Handbook for College Teachers.* 2nd ed. San Francisco: Jossey-Bass, 1993.

Bloom, B. S. (ed.). *Taxonomy of Educational Objectives: The Classification of Educational Goals.* New York: McKay, 1956.

Bransford, J. D., Brown, A. L., and Cocking, R. R. (eds.). *How People Learn: Brain, Mind, Experience, and School.* Washington, D.C.: National Academy Press, 2000.

Brown, J. S., Collins, A., and Duguid, P. "Situated Cognition and the Culture of Learning." *Educational Researcher,* 1989, *18,* 32–42.

Chickering, A. W. "Seven Principles for Good Practice in Undergraduate Education." In A. W. Chickering and Z. F. Gamson (eds.), *Applying the Seven Principles for Good Practice in Undergraduate Education.* New Directions for Teaching and Learning, no. 47. San Francisco: Jossey-Bass, 1991.

Cohen, S. A. "Instructional Alignment." *Educational Researcher,* 1987, *16*(8), 16–20.

DiPasquale, D. M., Mason, C. L., and Kolkhorst, F. W. "Exercise in Inquiry: Critical Thinking in an Inquiry-Based Exercise Physiology Laboratory Course." *Journal of College Science Teaching,* 2003, *32*(6), 388–393.

Donald, J. G. *Learning to Think.* San Francisco: Jossey-Bass, 2002.

Huber, M. T., and Morreale, S. P. (eds.). *Disciplinary Styles in the Scholarship of Teaching and Learning: Exploring Common Ground.* Washington, D.C.: American Association for Higher Education, 2002.

Hutchings, P., and Shulman, L. S. "The Scholarship of Teaching: New Elaborations, New Developments." *Change,* 1999, *31*(5), 10–15.

MacKinnon, G. R. "Why Models Sometimes Fail: Eight Suggestions to Improve Science Instruction." *Journal of College Science Teaching,* 2003, *32*(7), 430–433.

Michaelsen, L. "Three Keys to Using Learning Groups Effectively." *Essays on Teaching Excellence,* 1997, *9*(5), 1–2.

Perry, R., Menec, V., and Struthers, C. "Student Motivation from the Teacher's Perspective." In R. J. Menges and M. E. Weimer (eds.), *Teaching on Solid Ground: Using Scholarship to Improve Practice.* San Francisco: Jossey-Bass, 1995, pp. 75–100.

Shulman, L. "Knowledge and Teaching: Foundation of the New Reform." *Harvard Education Review,* 1987, *57,* 1–22.

Silberman, M. *Active Learning: 101 Strategies to Teach Any Subject.* Needham Heights, Mass.: Allyn & Bacon, 1996.

Smith, B., and MacGregor, J. "What Is Collaborative Learning?" In *Collaborative Learning: A Sourcebook for Higher Education.* University Park, Pa.: National Center on Postsecondary Teaching, Learning, and Assessment, 1992.

Svinicki, M. D. "New Directions in Learning and Motivation." In M. D. Svinicki (ed.), *Teaching and Learning on the Edge of the Millennium: Building on What We Have Learned.* New Directions for Teaching and Learning, no. 80. San Francisco: Jossey-Bass, 1999.

Tobias, S. "Disciplinary Cultures and General Education: What Can We Learn from Our Learners?" *Teaching Excellence,* 1992–1993, *4*(6), 1–3.

Wineburg, S. *Historical Thinking and Other Unnatural Acts: Charting the Future of Teaching the Past.* Philadelphia: Temple University Press, 2001.

Wright, D. "Using Learning Groups in Your Classroom: A Few How-to's." *Teaching at UNL Newsletter,* 1994, *15*(4), 1–2, 4–5.

Yuretich, R. F. "Encouraging Critical Thinking." *Journal of College Science Teaching,* 2004, *33*(3), 40–45.

JOAN MIDDENDORF *is codirector of the Faculty Learning Community at Campus Instructional Consulting, Indiana University.*

DAVID PACE *is associate professor of history and codirector of the Faculty Learning Community at Indiana University. He is also a fellow of the Carnegie Academy for the Scholarship of Teaching and Learning.*

2

*In most disciplines, professors ask students to "read"
without specifying what this operation means for their
particular field. This chapter traces the path laid out in a
cultural history class, where reading entails identifying
the essential elements of a text.*

Decoding the Reading of History: An Example of the Process

David Pace

There are few areas in which the differences in learning across academic disciplines are more visible than in that of reading. The instruction "read" has such a radically different meaning in the context of courses in physics, accounting, English, or history that we probably do students a disservice by even using the same word. This is a particularly difficult problem in history, where students often face hundreds of pages of reading and where several different forms of reading may be required in the same course. If college history teachers do not make some effort to teach the forms of reading necessary for their classes, it is likely that many students will be stopped at the beginning of the learning process.

Step 1. What Is the Bottleneck to Learning in This Class?

I began to grapple with this problem in the late 1980s and early 1990s (Pace, 1993) as my encounters with the scholarship in the field made me increasingly aware of the disciplinary nature of learning (see, for example, Brown, Collins, and Duguid, 1989; Tobias, 1992–1993). But I was only able to fully confront this challenge in the mid-1990s, when I set out to create from scratch a one hundred-student course on the history of ideas about the future for my university's freshman topics program.

My goal was to create a level playing field in which students who had weak backgrounds in historical thinking would have the same chance to master the material in the course as those who had been "preeducated." My previous experience as a teacher strongly suggested that I should focus a great deal of attention on the problems students face with reading. The most obvious problem was that of selectivity. Students lacked criteria for deciding what was most essential in a text and what could be passed over. Storytelling is essential to historical writing, but students tended to give the details the same attention as the broad outline of the story. For years I had heard students complain that they had difficulty remembering everything they had read. I had told them to concentrate on what was important, but I now recognize that this process of identifying the most important aspects of a text was a more complex task than I had realized and that I needed to show my students just how I went about this process.

Thus, my students' difficulty in distinguishing between the essential and the nonessential elements in a text was a clear bottleneck to learning in my course. This posed a problem for a large percentage of my students, and students found it difficult to master the basic elements of the course without having mastered this bottleneck. Therefore, I decided that this should be one of the central features around which I would shape the early weeks of the course.

Step 2. How Does an Expert Do These Things?

Before I could help students learn the specific forms of reading required in history courses, I had to reconstruct what professional historians do when they read secondary sources. This is a more difficult step than might be imagined because the process is so automatic to a trained historian that it is apt to be invisible. In retrospect, I can see that the process would have been greatly aided if I had then had access to the literature on reading in history at both the secondary and college levels that was just beginning to appear, in particular the research of Wineburg, who has marvelously demonstrated the intertextuality that lies at the core of so much of historical reading (Wineburg, 2001; Perfetti and others, 1994; Shemilt, 2000; Britt and others, 1994; McKeown and Beck, 1994). Lacking access to this literature at the time, I first tried introspection to get an idea of the steps that I, as a professional historian, take automatically when presented with a secondary source like those that my students struggle with. I also asked faculty members from history departments of my own and other universities just what they wanted students to do when they asked them to read particular passages.

From this, there emerged a series of steps by which expert historians organize a text as they read, separating what is essential from what is not:

They bring to the text a series of questions that need to be answered and add other questions as they arise from the process of reading.

They identify the central thesis and the subsidiary arguments that explain or qualify it.

They distinguish between these arguments and the evidence used to support them.

They commit to memory the central and the subsidiary arguments.
They retain selected bits of evidence to help them understand the nature of
the argument and ignore the rest.

This filtering process seems self-evident to professional historians, but
it is different from that used in other disciplines, and it is foreign to many
of those who take my courses. To students who read all the statements in a
secondary source as existing on the same level, none of this architecture
exists. They process the statement of the central thesis of a study in precisely the same manner as the least important piece of evidence, and the
task of memorization is enormous. Even if they are capable of such prodi-
gious acts of memory, they find that the mass of details is of little use in
completing the basic tasks of the course.

Step 3. How Can These Tasks Be Explicitly Modeled?

Because the ability to discriminate between essential and nonessential elements of a historical narrative is crucial to success in my course, I have
devoted a significant amount of energy to helping my students master this
ability during the first week. On the first day of class, I tell the students that
part of their job in college is to learn the specific forms of thinking that are
needed in each field in which they take courses. Then I describe history as
a storytelling discipline in which it is necessary to understand the point of
the story, not to memorize all of the details. I let them know that they will
need to be able to separate the broader story (or thesis) from the details that
support it; remember the story (or thesis) using the examples to confirm
that they understand the point; and forget most of the details, retaining only
a few well-chosen examples to help them remember the story and to allow
them to support the position if they need to. I show a passage from the
assigned readings in a PowerPoint slide and then show the same passage
again, but this time I have changed the font size of different phrases to indicate that for the purposes of our course, their importance determines their
size (see Figure 2.1).

After a discussion of why I made these particular choices, I pledge that
at no point in the course will they be asked a question that quizzes them on
details such as name five prophets in the *Old Testament*. A similar exercise,
involving collaborative learning teams, reinforces this learning in the second class period.

Because redundancy is an essential element in learning complex tasks,
I placed a parallel description of this process on the course Web site. But I
have also used the interactive potential of the Internet to model historical
reading in a more dynamic manner. On a second Web page, a student can
click on icons scattered across a passage from the week's readings and hear
a recording of what was going through my mind as I read that part of the
text. To give the listener a relatively unmediated experience of my reading

process, I intentionally recorded these comments without preparation or rehearsal and did not edit the hesitations and word choices. As I spoke, I was actually modeling several different aspects of historical reading, such as linking parts of this text to other texts or themes from the course. But the recording focused particularly on the process of establishing a hierarchy of importance in the text. To emphasize this point, I even indicated that, in the middle of an ancient Akkadian poem that had nothing to do with the issues in my course, I was going to skip to the end of that section without reading it all. (This and samples of other materials described in this chapter can be viewed at http://www.indiana.edu/~flp.)

Step 4. How Will Students Practice These Skills and Get Feedback?

Modeling the kinds of mental operations that are necessary for work in a discipline can be a crucial element in a systematic strategy for overcoming obstacles to student learning. But it is unlikely that these patterns of thinking will

Figure 2.1. Modeling Reading History Selectively

First overhead: A passage from the reading

"The Jewish apocalyptic genre emerged from the earlier prophetic tradition, but is distinct from it. The Jewish prophets of the eighth to the sixth centuries B.C.—Amos, Joel, Isaiah, Jeremiah, Ezekiel, and the others—functioned primarily as preachers, focusing on the people's transgressions and foretelling the Lord's renewed favor if they repented and further woes if they did not. The prophets were present minded and specific as they addressed a people beset by enemies and continually straying from the path of righteousness."

Second overhead: The same paragraph with the importance of difference sections emphasized:

"The Jewish apocalyptic genre emerged from the earlier prophetic tradition, but is distinct from it. The Jewish prophets of the eighth to the sixth centuries B.C.—Amos, Joel, Isaiah, Jeremiah, Ezekiel, and the others—functioned primarily as preachers, focusing on the people's transgressions and foretelling the Lord's renewed favor if they repented and further woes if they did not. The prophets were present minded and specific as they addressed a people beset by enemies and continually straying from the path of righteousness."

become part of students' cognitive repertoire unless they have opportunities to practice them and receive feedback. My course on the History of the Future provided this opportunity in two forms: in-class team exercises and online weekly assignments.

In the second class period, I reinforced the modeling of the previous meeting when I again gave the class another passage, but this time I asked them to decide in teams what parts are most and least important to remember and to articulate the principles that led to these judgments. The shared nature of this work not only forced students to make explicit the criteria that they use to establish a hierarchy of importance but also allowed me to provide them with extra feedback on how well they understood the process.

Ultimately, however, the students must learn to operate in the world of history on their own, and they need individual as well as group practice and feedback. Therefore, I have added to the course Web site weekly assignments modeled after Novak's *Just-in-Time Teaching* (Novak, Patterson, Gavrin, and Christian, 2004) that are targeted at specific operations that the students must master to succeed in the course. For example, in the first weekly Web assignment, students are given an additional passage from the readings and asked once again to specify one item from the text that they think they should not remember for the purposes of this course, to provide one item that they should remember, and to briefly explain both choices. In subsequent Web assignments, they are regularly asked to specify the central idea of a particular reading assignment, thus giving them more practice at distinguishing between essential statements of a thesis and supporting evidence.

These team and Web assignments serve to reinforce the basic patterns of historical reading that I have modeled in class, and they give the students feedback on their progress in this area. Thus, if students are at all engaged in the course, they should know well before the first exam whether their reading strategies are appropriate for this kind of course. At the same time, this work gives students an occasion to engage in some informal metacognitive explorations of how they used their minds in this and in other courses.

Step 5. What Will Motivate the Students?

This step of motivating students is absolutely crucial, and it needs to be considered carefully before the process of modeling, practice, and feedback begins. Students must be drawn willingly into this process of learning about learning, and it would be a serious error to assume that if we build a perfect pedagogical playing field, the students will automatically come along. They may need a special invitation.

Relatively few undergraduates conceive of their courses in terms of mastering different disciplinary ways of thinking, and they have to be shown that it is in their interest to spend time on this, rather than moving directly to "what will be on the test." I couch the presentation of the Decoding the Disciplines process (see Chapter One) in terms of students getting the maximum return on the time that they invest in a course. I point out that many surveys suggest that the difference between students who do well and those who do not is often more the result of how they study than of how much they study. I make it clear that a real commitment of time and energy is necessary for success, but that if they are not working in a manner that is appropriate to the discipline they are studying, more work is not apt to yield a higher grade.

The structure of the Decoding the Disciplines model itself can also make a positive contribution to motivation. It moves the focus from large, potentially overwhelming challenges, such as writing an essay exam, to more discrete and manageable tasks, such as deciding what is essential to remember in a passage of assigned reading. Students receive meaningful feedback each week on well-defined actions, rather than global feedback a few times during the course. Their sense of mastery can increase as they move to ever more complex tasks, and the learning environment is transformed from a few giant leaps to a series of manageable steps.

In addition, I present myself consistently as someone who wishes them to succeed and who has gone to considerable lengths to make it possible for them to master this material, regardless of their level of previous preparation. I mention my own difficulties as a first-generation college student moving from a substandard high school to a demanding college, and I stress that I have tried to create a course in which any student who has met the admissions requirements of my university should be able to succeed if she or he is willing to put in the work. But at the same time I make it clear that I have high expectations for them, that whereas the individual steps may be smaller, I expect them to make a real commitment to the process and to climb as high as or higher than students in other history classes.

Finally, I have placed this process of mastering historical thinking within an aesthetically pleasing and intellectually exciting context. The in-class work on these operations is accompanied by PowerPoint presentations that give visual learners an experience of the history of the future through images ranging from medieval frescos of the Apocalypse to science fiction covers from the 1920s. The weekly assignments are therefore part of a rich course Web site that gives students an experience of texts and images that reinforces this learning.

Step 6. How Well Are Students Mastering These Learning Tasks?

One of the great virtues of the Decoding the Disciplines model is that it makes assessment of student learning much simpler. When instructors attempt to measure global and often fuzzy concepts such as critical thinking, it is difficult to pinpoint which students have mastered the skills and which have not. In a history course, for example, a bad performance on an essay exam may be the result of a failure to master the grand concepts of the course or of an inability to operate on the much more basic level, such as knowing how to read in a manner appropriate to the discipline. Or a student may have mastered nine of ten essential skills, but the absence of the last one makes invisible the success that has been achieved.

The process of defining disciplinary operations brings precision to the process of assessment, and in most cases the mechanisms that give students an opportunity for practice and feedback can themselves provide useful information about where student learning is and is not occurring. This allows us to decide where to devote more of the precious class time to skills mastery and where that is less necessary.

As I have indicated earlier, in my course on the History of the Future, the team and Web exercises simultaneously help model basic operations, give the students practice at these operations, and serve to provide feedback. The results have been encouraging. Whereas in the past, a large number of my students in introductory courses remained unable to read secondary sources in a manner that is appropriate in a history course, now virtually the entire class demonstrates by the end of the first week that they can successfully discriminate the relative importance of different parts of the passage.

This exercise in prioritizing is not the end of the process because a number of other aspects of historical reading need to be taught later in the semester, and the basic patterns covered in the first week will need to be reinforced from time to time. But I can move forward in the knowledge that the great majority of the class will not be swamped in a sea of historical facts, all seemingly of equal importance.

It is also important to remember that this process does not—and in most cases should not—exclude more traditional methods of assessment. Students in my course write take-home essays in response to questions that I provide, just as they have always done in my classes. This provides them with an occasion to combine specific operations they have been learning in more complex tasks in a manner that more directly parallels the kinds of challenges they will be facing in later life. But now I can feel confident that if a student does badly, it is because he or she has not made a real commitment to the process, not because of a preexisting deficit of educational opportunity that my course is only compounding.

But what of content? In the case of the History of the Future course, what about changing patterns of thought, such as belief in the Apocalypse and secular progress, trust in technology and fear of nuclear devastation, the exclusion and inclusion of various groups in visions of the future, and all the other questions that arise when a historian looks at this material? What place has all of this content in a course that begins with step-by-step exercises in how to read history? I can slightly limit the effects of the time transferred from content to skills by being certain that the passages used in these exercises are particularly important to an understanding of the material because these are the sections of the readings that students are most apt to remember. But class time is limited, and the time spent on such exercises must be subtracted from time previously devoted directly to studying historical developments.

These are serious concerns, but ultimately these potential objections assume a kind of fetishistic relationship to teaching, as if the important event is what words pass through my mouth, not what new ideas enter my students' brains. In fact, the only thing that really matters is what happens in the minds of students. If my students do not understand the basic language of history, my presentations are as pointless as if they were delivered in ancient Akkadian. Absolutely nothing real has been lost if the content that has been sacrificed was not being understood in the first place.

In the past, I was faced with a chilling choice between teaching to the small portion of the class that had already been preeducated in the craft of history or of lowering the level of instruction to a flat recitation of facts. I now feel that I have tools that can give me the ability to open the discussion to students who would otherwise never have access to the great banquet of knowledge and insight that contemporary historiography can offer them. If I can expand the number of students who can be invited to this banquet by even a few percentage points each semester, it is a small price to pay for a diversion of a small portion of the time I share with them.

References

Britt, A. M, Georgi, M. C., Perfetti, C. A., and Rouet, J. F. "Learning from History Texts: From Causal Analysis to Argument Models." In G. Leinhardt, I. L. Beck, and C. Stainton (eds.), *Teaching and Learning in History*. Hillsdale, N.J.: Erlbaum, 1994, pp. 47–84.

Brown, J. S., Collins A., and Duguid, P. "Situated Cognition and the Culture of Learning," *Educational Researcher*, 1989, *13*, 32–41.

McKeown, M. G., and Beck, I. L. "Making Sense of Accounts of History: Why Don't They and How They Might." In G. Leinhardt, I. L. Beck, and C. Stainton (eds.), *Teaching and Learning in History*. Hillsdale, N.J.: Erlbaum, 1994, pp. 1–26.

Novak, G. M., Patterson, E. T., Gavrin, A. D., and Christian, W. *Just-in-Time Teaching: Blending Active Learning with Web Technology*. Upper Saddle River, N.J.: Prentice Hall, 2004.

Pace, D. "Beyond 'Sorting': Teaching Cognitive Skills in the History Survey." *History Teacher*, 1993, 26(4), 211–220.

Perfetti, C. A., and others. "How Students Use Texts to Learn and Reason About Historical Uncertainty." In M. C. Voss and J. F. Voss (eds.), *Cognitive and Instructional Processes in History and the Social Sciences*. Hillsdale, N.J.: Erlbaum, 1994, pp. 257–283.

Shemilt, D. "The Caliph's Coin: The Currency of Narrative Frameworks in History Teaching." In P. N. Stearns, P. Seixas, and S. Wineburg (eds.), *Knowing, Teaching, and Learning History: National and International Perspectives*. New York: New York University Press, 2000, pp. 83–101.

Tobias, S. "Disciplinary Cultures and General Education: What Can We Learn from Our Learners?" *Teaching Excellence,* 1992–1993, 4(6), 1–3.

Wineburg, S. *Historical Thinking and Other Unnatural Acts: Charting the Future of Teaching the Past.* Philadelphia: Temple University Press, 2001.

DAVID PACE *is associate professor of history and codirector of the Faculty Learning Community at Indiana University. He is also a fellow of the Carnegie Academy for the Scholarship of Teaching and Learning.*

3

For three biology professors, visualizing molecular processes is central to thinking in their discipline. This chapter reports their attempts at getting students to make this same cognitive move and the results of their assessments.

Decoding Genetics and Molecular Biology: Sharing the Movies in Our Heads

Miriam Zolan, Susan Strome, Roger Innes

As classroom teachers in biology, we struggle with the proper balance of content versus process. We teach an information-rich science that is expanding exponentially. Yet, most faculty would agree that the average biology student has trouble understanding fundamental biological processes such as meiosis (the segregation of chromosomes into sperm and egg cells) and gene regulation (how genes are turned on and off). Because these processes are complex, we typically ask our students to learn many specific details about them, but simply learning the details does not necessarily lead to a true understanding of how a process works. Showing lots of pictures in class and explaining a process in great detail during a lecture does not seem to give students practice in the kinds of thinking we expect them to learn.

Partly because of these frustrations, several members of the biology faculty at Indiana University, including the three of us, have been investigating alternatives to standard lecture formats for teaching biology. We encountered the Decoding the Disciplines model (see Chapter One) as fellows in our university's Faculty Learning Community. Using this approach, we began by each defining a bottleneck that our students faced. Although the three of us defined our bottlenecks differently and came up with different solutions, in retrospect we were all trying to overcome a similar problem: how to get our students to move beyond the memorization of facts to a deeper understanding of biological processes.

The next step in the Decoding the Disciplines approach was to define the steps that we, as professional scientists, would use to overcome the challenges that limit our students' learning. This led to the realization that in response to the kinds of problems contained in all three bottlenecks, we usually develop a kind of dynamic movie or cartoon in our minds that organizes the information we currently have and helps us make a guess (hypothesis) about how the process might work. We also realized that we were not explicitly developing such model-building skills in our students and that this was an essential skill for making sense of the vast array of information we present to them.

To address this problem, each of us independently developed some form of hands-on modeling exercise (step 3 of Decoding the Disciplines) that required students to manipulate objects to illustrate a process. We found that it was not enough for us to demonstrate biological processes; we had to help students develop the dynamic cartoons we use in our minds. Furthermore, we learned that students could develop their skill at this kind of visualization using kinesthetic props (MacKinnon, 2003). Following this modeling step, we gave students ample opportunity to practice these skills, to receive feedback (step 4), and to use such opportunities as a tool for testing their own understanding of the process. We motivated our students through exercises that were kinesthetically appealing and gave them a sense of self-efficacy. Before setting the students loose on these exercises, we explicitly told them what we were trying to accomplish by having them create these models and how we hoped it would facilitate their learning (step 5). Finally, we assessed the results of these efforts regularly across the semester, often using Classroom Assessment Techniques (CATs) borrowed from Angelo and Cross (1993). Below, each of us describes our specific modeling exercise, and our assessment of its effectiveness.

Problem-Based Learning in the Study of Mitosis and Meiosis (Zolan)

As part of the introductory course for biology majors, I cover the cell divisions of mitosis and meiosis, with an emphasis on chromosome segregation. The bottleneck I addressed was that students do not have a clear understanding of mitosis and meiosis. They have encountered the terms in previous (high school) classes and do not really listen when they are supposed to be investigating them again. They also have trouble distinguishing between identical (sister chromatids) and similar chromosomes (homologs). The lack of a firm understanding of these processes makes it difficult for students when they later study genetics.

My traditional method of teaching mitosis and meiosis was to draw out the cell divisions in lecture, show how they are the basis for eukaryotic genetics, and then reinforce the descriptions with some demonstrations using pipe cleaner models. Unfortunately, this did not prove to be sufficient for my students to be able to visualize this dynamic process in the manner that I and other biologists do (MacKinnon, 2003). Therefore, I decided to flip my approach and use an inquiry-based learning strategy wherein students would "invent" mitosis and meiosis by working with simple pipe cleaner models.

Description of the First Class Session. As the approximately 250 students in my course entered the classroom for the first lecture on this material, they picked up two red and two white pipe cleaners, each of which had a piece of blank tape attached. After I defined some terms for the students, they labeled one of the red "chromosomes" with a bead marker, representing an allele of the ABO blood group locus. I asked the class for the possible choices, and students eagerly volunteered because it was something they confidently knew. They then labeled one of their white pipe cleaners with an allele for an Rh factor gene, after a similar discussion of choices.

I then asked students whether their chromosome complement would make up a haploid or a diploid cell. After they correctly identified their chromosome complement as haploid, students then "mated" their two chromosomes with those of a neighbor to create a diploid cell. I talked about genotype and phenotype and then had partners work together to decide the genotype of their cell, whether it was heterozygous or homozygous for the two genes, and what the phenotypes of the cell were for these traits. As a class, we then built up genotype-phenotype charts for both genes and defined dominance and codominance.

Next, I asked students to discuss with their partners how to start with one of them holding all the chromosomes used so far and end with both of them having a complete chromosome set. I reminded them that they could use additional pipe cleaners. I told them to think about what mitosis does, what it needs, and how it might work. As students worked in pairs or small groups, I circulated among them and helped them get started. After students had worked together, I asked for volunteers to explain what they had done and helped students bring out the two important features: DNA replication and separation of sister chromatids into the two products of mitosis.

In the future, I will have undergraduate instructors circulate during the lessons, preventing students from using the size of a large class to avoid active participation in the exercise. Students might also be asked to sit with their own learning groups to minimize their anonymity.

When the students next met with their weekly learning groups, they were asked to repeat the process of mitosis (step 4 in the Decoding the Disciplines model), to draw chromosomes at different stages of the mitotic cell cycle, to use pipe cleaners to illustrate meiosis, and then to mate the resulting haploid products to create new diploid individuals.

Assessment. Before the lessons began, students took a multiple-choice pretest that asked them to classify four pictures as representative of particular phases of mitosis or meiosis. After the lessons, students were again asked to classify five similar pictures as particular phases of mitosis or meiosis. In this post-test, a fourth category, "does not represent a stage of normal mitosis or meiosis," was added to the multiple-choice answers, and a fifth picture, which was not a possible stage of either process, was also added. Figure 3.1 shows the percentages of students correctly identifying

Figure 3.1. Assessment of Problem-Based Learning of Mitosis Versus Meiosis

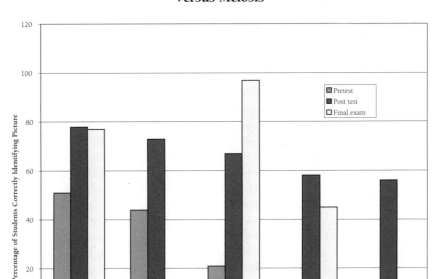

the pictures in the pretest and post-test and their scores on two of the same questions on the final exam seven weeks later. It is clear that more students were able to correctly identify the pictures in the post-test than in the pretest.

My Evaluation of the Process. This process was valuable because it turned a study of mitosis and meiosis on its head (by having students "invent" these processes rather than listening to a lecture about them) and allowed the students and me to see what they do and do not understand.

Modeling Chromosomes and Genetic Processes (Strome)

I teach a course in genetics to sophomore and junior-level students. Understanding how chromosomes and the genes that reside on them behave during mitosis and meiosis is at the heart of almost all concepts that we study in genetics. A bottleneck that I have faced over the years is the difficulty students have visualizing chromosomes, appreciating the distinction between similar and identical chromosomes (for example, homologs and sister chromatids), and predicting their segregation patterns during mitosis and meiosis. My goals were to develop easy-to-manipulate, three-dimensional representations of chromosomes and genes and to have the students model their behavior during mitosis and meiosis and during other genetic events.

Representing Chromosomes and Genes with Pipe Cleaners and Beads. The first day of class, I used the "background knowledge probe" CAT (Angelo and Cross, 1993) to find out what students already knew about chromosomes. The students' answers clearly showed that there was a lot of confusion about the definition of a chromosome and the distinction between homologs and sister chromatids. I explained that we would model chromosomes using pipe cleaners and model genes using beads. Pipe cleaners and beads allow visualization of which chromosomes are identical, which chromosomes are similar, and which chromosomes are completely different.

To convey what *identical, similar,* and *different* mean for chromosomes, I used the simple genetic system of the fruit fly. Fruit fly cells, with two each of only four different chromosomes, are easy to model with pipe cleaners: two blue, two yellow, two green, and two red pipe cleaners (Figure 3.2). Genes were represented as colored beads, which I strung on the pipe cleaners to represent either different genes (pairs of beads both the same pattern or shade of gray in the figure)) or different forms of a particular gene (single pair of beads that are different shades in the figure). Students could see from the lineup of beads on the two red pipe cleaners that those "chromosomes" were similar (homologs) but not identical. For simplicity, I stripped off all but the purple and aqua beads, leaving those to mark and track the homologs during mitosis and meiosis. I used our pipe cleaners and beads to model the exact duplication of chromosomes, which is the first step in mitosis and meiosis. This created identical chromosomes (sister chromatids), as shown in Figure 3.2.

Students were then given their own sets of pipe cleaners and beads and asked to work together to model the different ways that chromosomes can align in preparation for cell division. Students discovered for themselves how different chromosome alignments lead to different outcomes during mitosis and meiosis.

We used pipe cleaners and beads throughout the semester to model a number of important concepts in genetics (see http://www.indiana.edu/~flp). An important component of all of our discussions was following up on our pipe cleaner and bead work by devising two-dimensional representations of chromosomes and genes for students' notes. We usually used different-colored lines for different chromosomes and standard genetic symbols for different forms of a particular gene. We went back and forth frequently between drawings and pipe cleaners to help students consolidate what they had learned and to ensure that they understood the different representations. In the process, my students internalized the visualization processes that are automatic to biologists and necessary for understanding biology.

Assessment. To gauge students' understanding of chromosomes and their ability to apply that understanding to new situations, I posed questions

Figure 3.2. Modeling Fruit Fly Chromosomes Using Pipe Cleaners and Beads

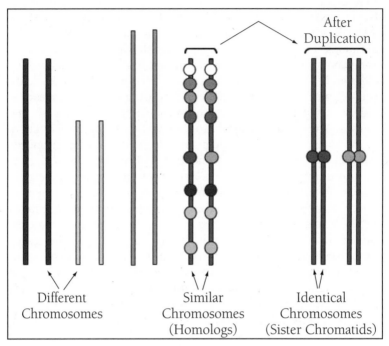

in class and asked students to work in groups of two or three and hold up their group answer as pipe cleaners and beads for the class to see. If one or only a few groups figured out the correct answer, they explained their answer to the rest of the class. This polling was informative because it showed me immediately what percentage of groups came up with correct arrangements of pipe cleaners and beads, and more important, it showed the ways in which some arrangements were incorrect. That enabled me to focus on each group's misconception(s).

I also used a CAT known as "Conceptest" (Ellis, Landis, and Meeker, n.d.) where I had students work together to solve chromosome-based problems and then asked them to vote for one of several answers. If a significant fraction of the class missed the problem, I asked them to resume discussion and then vote again. After the second round of discussion, I sometimes asked students with a firm grasp of the concept to explain their logic to those who were still confused.

One question on exam 1 tested the students' ability to draw, organize, and correctly label meiotic chromosomes. Sixty-six percent of students answered this question correctly. Exams 2 and 3 each had a "chromosome basics" question as part of a bigger problem to solve. The percentage of students who drew and labeled chromosomes correctly was 73 percent and 71 percent, respectively.

My Evaluation. I think that most students benefited from seeing me consistently use pipe cleaners and beads, either projected onto a screen by way of a document camera or held up as I circulated through the class. However, it turned out to be awkward to have the students use pipe cleaners and beads in class, in large part because the desktops in the class were too small to accommodate both notes and learning kits. Having students sit at tables would be preferred (Wood, 2003) because it would allow them to lay out and manipulate their chromosome sets while still being able to talk with each other and take notes. In fact, during office hours and when talking with students after class, we often used pipe cleaner models on a desk or tabletop. As students set up and worked through different scenarios, I was treated to a few "eureka" moments as students connected our pipe cleaner-and-bead exercises with their prior knowledge and with concepts presented in class. I will definitely continue to use pipe cleaners and beads, but in the future I will modify how I ask the students to work with them, perhaps by moving some of their hands-on pipe cleaner and bead work to the small-group discussion sessions that meet each week to work on problem sets.

Using Our Bodies to Model Molecular Processes (Innes)

I have been teaching molecular biology and genetics at the university level for the past thirteen years and during this time have been continually impressed by the disconnect between the ability of most students to learn long lists of "facts" (quite good) and their ability to use these facts to understand how a particular process works in space and time (very poor). For example, a process that I feel is central to molecular biology is how a gene is "turned on" at the right place and right time. This is a complex process that requires an understanding of protein structure and interactions among various proteins and between proteins and DNA. Although students readily learned the names of specific proteins and DNA sequences that are involved in this process, exam questions that moved beyond simple regurgitation of facts revealed that most students were failing to understand how the process actually worked. On discussing this bottleneck with a nonscientist colleague, I realized that part of my students' difficulties might stem from their lack of practice with thinking of biological information in terms of animated processes. Perhaps my students were not routinely painting pictures in their minds that organized information in terms of a cartoon. I therefore developed an exercise that made such modeling an explicit part of the learning process, with two goals in mind: to demonstrate to students the value of modeling so that they would apply this approach to other learning situations and to use modeling to demonstrate how both space and time are key aspects of understanding a process.

Although my ultimate goal was to get the students to create cartoons in their mind's eye, I decided I needed to start with something more concrete and accessible. I wanted an exercise that would force them to think in terms of real space and real time, an exercise that would force them to answer questions such as, "How do particular proteins interact? How does the process occur in space? What would happen to the process if a particular protein was missing? Do I have enough information to understand the function of each protein in the process? If not, what other information do I need?" In one of the first classes of the semester, I explicitly told the students that I organized information and developed new questions for my own research by creating a model of a biological process and that I wanted them to start doing the same. In other words, I wanted them to "think like a scientist."

Ultimately, I decided that the best way to get students thinking about these questions was to have the students "become" the proteins and act out the process using the "class modeling" CAT (Angelo and Cross, 1993). Using class modeling allows students to assimilate information in a kinesthetic way (Gardner, 1993) and increases their motivation. As a test case, I chose to have the students act out the basics of how a steroid hormone (such as testosterone) turns on specific genes.

After a brief discussion and overview of the process, I asked the students (I had only four in my class) to form a single team, and I gave them a short set of written instructions. I listed four major protein players in the process by which testosterone turns on a gene and asked the students to each become one of these proteins. I also gave them a specific DNA sequence to which the protein complex would bind. Their task was then to model each of the events associated with turning on the gene in the correct temporal sequence and to interact with each other as the actual proteins would. I taped up a long roll of paper towels around the classroom on which a long DNA sequence was written. Thus, the students had to search for the correct sequence as part of the process. As one can imagine, much giggling was associated with the exercise, but it forced the students to think about the sequential order of events and to discuss with each other exactly how the process worked.

Assessment. The first level of assessment was simply observing how the students performed in their attempts at three-dimensional modeling with themselves as parts. This provided me with immediate feedback on what they had understood from my presentation and where they were confused. The more important assessment, however, was an assessment technique that I invented and called the "storyboard" CAT. I asked them to draw a cartoon, using symbols to represent the various proteins, of a similar gene activation event. I also asked them to provide a key to explain their symbols and a brief explanation of each panel. My goal here was to determine whether they could transfer what they had learned from the dynamic three-dimensional modeling that we had done in class to a static two-dimensional drawing similar to what is found in most textbooks; the students were successful at this task.

I also asked them to identify one step in this process in which the mechanism was unclear and write a specific question that they would like answered about this step, in an adaptation of the "muddiest point" CAT (Angelo and Cross, 1993). By having students formulate questions, they discovered that they could use model building to help them identify what they did *not* know. I was pleased by the questions that the students came up with because they displayed a relatively sophisticated level of understanding. Most were questions that we do not yet have the answer to, which provided an excellent starting point for a follow-up discussion.

In summary, I thought the combination of modeling a molecular biology process using the students' own bodies, along with a later reconstruction of the model on paper, was an effective learning exercise. The only downside is that this activity would be challenging to accomplish in a large lecture room with dozens of students. It could, however, be adapted to such a class through the fishbowl technique (Silberman, 1996) in which a group of students would take on the roles of the proteins in front of the whole class and the audience would tell the actors where they should go and what they should do. As a follow-up, all of the students could then perform a similar exercise in their weekly learning group in which three or four groups could do this at the same time.

Because I have not yet applied this approach in a large lecture class, I do not have any data comparing its effectiveness with standard lecture-only methods. Based on how engaged the students were, however, I firmly believe that student understanding of how genes are turned on was much improved.

Discussion

We all found that the hands-on activities we used were highly effective in three ways. First, they helped our students' understanding of the specific concepts we were trying to teach. Second, they helped the students and us to see students' misconceptions and thus address them. Third, and most important, they helped our students learn the essential skill of visualizing biological processes.

An additional critical observation we made was that although we developed our activities for different class sizes, we found that each can be adapted for use in a different setting. For example, Zolan found that the problem-based learning approach to mitosis and meiosis was ideal for an upper-level course with an enrollment of about twenty-five students; in this setting, she could interact personally with all the students. Strome used the fishbowl technique (Silberman, 1996) to employ Innes's activity in her one hundred-student class and found it highly effective. Innes took Strome's pipe cleaner and bead kits into his small class and found them useful for helping students to master the connection between the mathematical predictions of genetic inheritance and their physical underpinnings in chromosome movements. Thus, we are enthusiastic about what we see as the next extension of our work, the creation of a "toolkit" of ideas and activities that our colleagues can use in their own classes. (Specific material for each of our activities can be found at the Web site given earlier.) Activities for stimulating student inquiry and engagement can be introduced into a classroom at the level of between one and four per semester; it is not necessary to completely revamp an existing course all at once for the impact on student learning to be substantial (Pukkila, 2004).

References

Angelo, T. A., and Cross, K. P. *Classroom Assessment Techniques: A Handbook for College Teachers.* 2nd ed. San Francisco: Jossey-Bass, 1993.

Ellis, A. B., Landis, C. R., and Meeker, K. "Classroom Assessment Techniques Concept Tests" [online]. n.d. Madison: University of Wisconsin. http://www.flaguide.org/cat/contests/contests1.php. Accessed June 17, 2004.

Gardner, H. *Frames of Mind: The Theory of Multiple Intelligences.* New York: Basic Books, 1993.

MacKinnon, G. R. "Why Models Sometimes Fail: Eight Suggestions to Improve Science Instruction." *Journal of College Science Teaching,* 2003, *32*(7), 430–433.

Pukkila, P. J. "Introducing Student Inquiry in Large Introductory Genetics Classes." *Genetics,* 2004, *166,* 11–18.

Silberman, M. *Active Learning: 101 Strategies to Teach Any Subject.* Needham Heights, Mass.: Allyn & Bacon, 1996.

Wood, W. B. "Inquiry-Based Undergraduate Teaching in the Life Sciences at Large Research Universities: A Perspective on the Boyer Commission Report." *Cell Biology Education,* 2003, *2,* 112–116.

MIRIAM ZOLAN is professor in the Department of Biology at Indiana University.

SUSAN STROME is professor in the Department of Biology at Indiana University.

ROGER INNES is professor in the Department of Biology at Indiana University.

4

Two astronomy professors, using the Decoding the Disciplines process, help their students use abstract theories to analyze light and to visualize the enormous scale of astronomical concepts.

Decoding Astronomical Concepts

Richard H. Durisen, Catherine A. Pilachowski

Familiar refrains from nonscience majors taking introductory astronomy classes are, "This stuff is too difficult for a 100-level class," and "I usually get As, but I've been studying harder for this class than any other, and I still have a D!" Many students at the freshman level do not realize that modern astronomy is a rigorous physical science, not just the "naming of stars" or the taking of pretty Hubble Space Telescope pictures. Contemporary astronomy is more properly called *astrophysics,* literally, the study of the "nature" of celestial objects, what they are like physically and how they behave. Even a descriptive treatment of an object invokes unfamiliar concepts from all areas of science, and it involves exotic phenomena and mind-bogglingly enormous scales that stretch the imaginations of the astronomers themselves.

One advantage we have over many other freshman-level introductory science offerings is that there is no part of astronomy that our students *must* know. This allows us freedom to experiment with content and methods, although it brings a concomitant responsibility to offer students an informative and exciting glimpse of not only what we know about the universe around us but also how we know it.

In this chapter, we discuss our efforts to overcome common bottlenecks to learning in astronomy courses. The bottleneck described by the first author (Durisen) concerns difficulties students have in understanding how the analysis of light is used to extract useful astronomical information and their more general failure to grasp how astronomical knowledge is constructed. The second author (Pilachowski) then discusses the second bottleneck, which involves helping students visualize astronomical concepts.

NEW DIRECTIONS FOR TEACHING AND LEARNING, no. 98, Summer 2004 © Wiley Periodicals, Inc.

Spectrum Analysis and the Nature of Scientific Inquiry (Durisen)

Many students act as if modern ideas about our universe are revealed to astronomers simply by looking through ever-more-powerful·telescopes. They do not appreciate the generations of meticulous observation and reasoning required to produce this knowledge. Specifically, they do not realize that apart from studies of meteorites and cosmic rays and data from spacecraft sent to solar system objects, the vast bulk of astronomical information about the universe comes from the analysis of light. Such analysis allows us to determine properties of celestial objects such as their composition, temperature, density, their speed of motion toward or away from us, and much more. Without some understanding of this technique, students might think that astronomers make up this amazing stuff out of thin air, rather than deduce it from painstaking dissection and interpretation of the dim light reaching us from the far-away universe.

Nature of the Bottleneck. I describe my efforts to overcome two related bottlenecks to learning: a narrower but essential one concerning how the light spectra of distant objects can be used to deduce important information (such as the presence of planets around stars) and a broader, more fundamental bottleneck about understanding how astronomers create knowledge. Beneath both of these lies a deeper problem: the difficulty most students have in grasping abstract models used to explain complex physical phenomena and in understanding how such theoretical models are extracted from empirical data.

Most elementary college astronomy textbooks foster these bottlenecks by describing spectrum analysis through a top-down approach in which abstract concepts and theoretical models from physics on the nature of light and matter are presented as givens. The consequences for spectrum analysis in astronomy are then deduced as practical applications. During two decades of following this approach, I found it to be the low point of student interest and performance. They just did not "get it." Reflecting on this during an Indiana University Faculty Learning Community (IUFLC) workshop, I suspected that many of my nonscience students became confused and frustrated because they could not make the series of conceptual steps from the theoretical model to practical applications. On deeper reflection, I realized the obvious: the top-down approach was in fact terribly unscientific! Theoretical models are distilled from analysis of empirical data, not the other way around. Worse yet, by using only lecture plus demonstration, I was talking "at" them, both literally and conceptually.

A "Historical" Approach with a Practical Focus. In the fall 2003 semester, I taught a small freshman seminar class of twenty students and decided to take a different tact. I made three changes. First, I introduced spectrum analysis in the context of a specific application. My seminar was called "The Search for Habitable Planets," and so one fundamental question for this class was, "How do we detect planets around other stars?" Second, to help my students understand how this knowledge was generated, I patterned my development of the subject along historical lines, rather than giving them the "correct" physics story from the beginning. Finally, I used interactive techniques (Hake, 1998) and short-answer assessment tools (Angelo and Cross, 1993; Ellis, Landis, and Meeker, n.d.), following steps 4 and 6 in the Decoding the Disciplines model. (PowerPoint slides for the class sessions can be found at http://www.indiana.edu/~flp.)

Initial Concept Inventory. To increase student learning and to model the process of scientific inquiry, we began with their input, not mine. I began by asking the students to put themselves in the mindset of nineteenth-century astronomers and posed the question, "What might they want to know about stars?" Inevitably, students came up with, among others, two key focus questions: "What are stars made of?" and "Do they have planets?" At this point, I reminded them that all we have to work with is the light we receive from stars. Before I launched into any lecturing about light, students completed a Classroom Assessment Technique (CAT) called "background knowledge probe" (Angelo and Cross, 1993) by answering the question, "What are some properties of light?" For these and other assessments, Scott Michael, an Indiana University astronomy graduate student and experienced teaching assistant, evaluated the students' responses.

Figure 4.1 shows a histogram of the number of students with varying numbers of correct concepts about light. Results were better than I expected. Only two of nineteen students responding had no accurate knowledge about light whereas many already had some conceptual framework on which to build.

After spending some time bringing all students up to a common knowledge base about properties of light, I confronted them, through lecture and demonstrations, with a central puzzle of nineteenth-century physics and astrophysics, namely, that different elements emit and absorb only certain definite wavelengths (energies, colors) of light. The next assessment was directed at three issues: comprehension of material up to that point, the efficacy of group work, and competence at theoretical model building. I used the following "focused listing" CAT (Angelo and Cross, 1993), "Given what you now know about light, what do 'spectral lines' tell you about how matter emits and absorbs light? Devise a theory of the structure of atoms that can explain this phenomenon." I asked them to answer this question in writing both before and after discussion in small groups.

As shown in Figure 4.2, group discussion improved understanding about spectral lines. Wrong answers decreased from seven to five, and partially correct answers went up dramatically. On the other hand, as evidenced by Figure 4.3, student efforts to devise a theory were mostly unsuccessful, and group discussion produced only marginal improvements. With only two or three exceptions, students at best tended to parrot an empirical description of phenomena as their "theory." Probably like most

Figure 4.1. Student Knowledge About Light

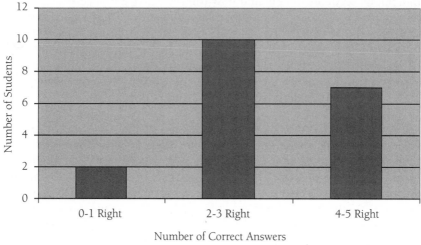

Number of Correct Answers

Figure 4.2. Before (Light Gray) and After (Dark Gray) Group Work: Spectral Lines

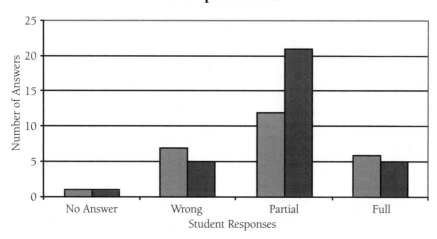

Student Responses

human beings, these freshmen were good at grasping empirical information but had little idea how to abstract in the manner of an astrophysicist.

These results reinforce the importance of steps 4 and 6 of the Decoding the Disciplines model (Chapter One). Students cannot be expected to "theorize" in physics or astronomy without being given an opportunity to practice disciplinary ways of thinking with feedback (step 4). In the future, it would probably be helpful for me to model the process explicitly and to guide the students to the specific theory more gradually, using a series of

Figure 4.3. Devising a Theory of Matter Before (Light Gray) and After (Dark Gray) Group Work

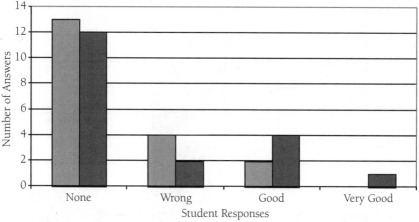

leading questions with feedback. Assessments (step 6) are necessary to know what is and is not working and to adjust efforts accordingly.

A Practical Problem: Detection of Extrasolar Planets. After some lecture and discussion concerning the theory of how matter emits and absorbs light, I moved on to the practical question, "How do we discover extrasolar planets?" It was then necessary to discuss the Doppler Effect. After solicitation of students' input and some lecture clarification, I asked them to answer another background knowledge probe: "Given the information you now have about light, how might we analyze the light from stars to detect extrasolar planets?" Again, they answered this question before and after a discussion in small groups. Of course, I had a preconceived notion of the "right" answer (the most successful planet discovery technique), namely, detection of periodic Doppler shifts in the spectral lines of stars due to their back-and-forth motion in response to the gravitational force of an orbiting planet. As shown in Figure 4.4, there were few fully correct answers, with little improvement after discussion in small groups. My interpretation is that there were still too many abstract conceptual steps for most students to make, even with the benefit of peer discussion.

On the other hand, I unexpectedly found, to my delight, that if I made allowances for imprecision, the students actually ended up proposing just about every method for planet detection that has actually been attempted! This is reflected in Figure 4.4 by the large number of responses labeled "partially" correct. When the challenge was concrete, the students were reasonably good at inventing applications for the concepts we had developed. I adjusted my lecture (Novak, Patterson, Gavrin, and Christian, 1999) to correspond to the outcome of this assessment, sharing the merits of their partially correct answers, and went over the Doppler shift-detection method.

Figure 4.4. Responses Before (Light Gray) and After (Dark Gray) Group Work: Detecting Extrasolar Planets

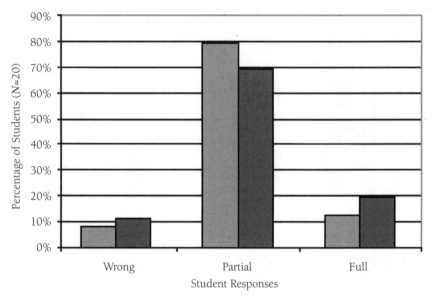

As a final in-class assessment, I had the students describe extrasolar planet detection in the "one-sentence summary" CAT (Angelo and Cross, 1993), "Who does what to whom (or what), when, where, why, and how?" Fifteen students uniformly gave good concrete, practical descriptions of the Doppler shift method ("what," fifteen students; "to what," fifteen; and "why," fourteen). They were still not as good at providing abstract explanations of "how" the technique works (twelve students), and because I did not emphasize the human activity of science, they often left out "who" (eight students), "when" (none), and "where" (seven).

Successes, Failures, and Revelations. In the end, I discovered that the students in my seminar began the course with useful fragments of information about light (Figure 4.1) on which an instructor could build. They not only could comprehend (Figure 4.2) but were actually good at inventing (Figure 4.4) complex applications of empirical physics to a practical problem, even though they were weaker in their ability to create abstract theoretical models (Figure 4.3) and to offer abstract theoretical reasons. All in all, I was satisfied with the outcome. It is no surprise that young nonscience majors have difficulty with abstract theoretical models. Perhaps at this level of instruction, what is more important is their evident and, to me surprising, ability to use practical, empirical rules of behavior in a creative way (Figure 4.4) when asked to do so. This reflects a path of success in conveying useful information and reinforcing desirable patterns of thinking. I concluded that if I want more students to be able to create and use abstract models, I have to spend more time on model building and guiding them to a specific model in smaller, digestible steps.

Grappling with Visualization in Astronomy (Pilachowski)

Students in introductory astronomy classes confront sizes and distances that are much too large to relate to their everyday lives, and they find difficulty in organizing information about the structures we find in the universe. For example, misconceptions about the relative sizes of the earth and moon and the distance between them and about the relative sizes of the solar system and the galaxy are common. Visualization is therefore important throughout the course as we study the relationships between and the evolution of astronomical bodies (Straits and Wilke, 2003). Unless students can shift perspective to visualize celestial objects from other points of view, they are unable to understand or learn about the causes of the various celestial and astrophysical phenomena.

Nature of the Bottleneck. Astronomers use several methods to assist with visualization tasks, including diagrams, three-dimensional models, and mathematical models (Bransford, Brown, and Cocking, 2000). Astronomy textbooks also include many schematic diagrams to illustrate astrophysical concepts. To a scientist, these diagrams contain the kernels of astrophysical concepts, and the text serves primarily to flesh out the idea with further detail. We look first at the diagrams to understand the ideas and only secondarily read the text to fill in those details. Most nonscience students, however, focus first on the text and lose the central idea in the myriad details they find there. Their experience in other courses often leads them to see illustrations and images as decoration or enrichment rather than as primary content. Therefore, it is necessary to develop ways to model this process of "thinking visually" to help students identify and master critical astronomy concepts more easily.

Modeling the Visualization of the Earth-Moon System. Students' first challenge in thinking visually in an astronomy course generally comes with an introduction to the night sky. A bottleneck occurs when we move from the simple description of the phenomena in the sky (identifying constellations, the rising and setting of the sun) to a three-dimensional visualization to explain why the phenomena happen as they do. This visualization often involves moving one's perspective from a spot on earth to a view seen from elsewhere in the solar system.

Visualization of the earth-moon system provides students with a comfortable place to begin. We provide balls of different sizes and a large ball in the center of the room simulating the sun and ask students, working in small groups, to estimate what time the moon will rise when the earth and moon are placed in particular configurations. Once they have mastered this concept, they then reverse the process to determine where the moon must be, relative to the earth and sun, when the moon rises at a particular time. Photographs of the moon showing its phase and location in the sky are displayed (for example, Ansel Adams's photo *Moonrise, Hernandez,* and an image of a space shuttle launch from Cape Canaveral) are displayed, and students are asked to determine the orientation of the earth and moon when the photograph was taken.

Practice and Feedback. It is rarely sufficient to model a complex process once. Therefore, students were provided with several drawings of the earth and moon at different times during the lunar month and asked to sketch the phase of the moon and to estimate the time it will rise. Students worked in class while the instructors circulated among them to answer questions and provide encouragement. Instructors also assessed how well students are able to shift perspective to understand and reproduce earth-moon orientations and to predict when the moon will rise and what its phase will be. Students then complete their work outside of class. Although this exercise does help the students learn about the earth-moon system, including the relative sizes and separation of the two bodies, its main purpose is to help them begin to visualize bodies in three dimensions.

Assessment of Learning. In a class of 220 students, analysis of completed student worksheets indicated that 73 percent of students were able to determine the time of moonrise from a diagram showing the relative orientation of the earth, moon, and sun whereas only 44 percent were able to predict the phase of the moon (full, gibbous, half, crescent, or new). Others (43 percent) found the task so daunting that they did not attempt to complete this portion of the (ungraded) worksheet. Of the 98 students who attempted to predict the phases of the moon, 78 percent did so correctly.

Cycling Back Through Modeling and Practicing Visualization. As these figures indicate, visualization is a complex process, and many students can master it only by passing through a number of such learning opportunities. Therefore, throughout the course we continued to provide students with opportunities in class to practice and develop visualization skills and encouraged them to use everyday objects as three-dimensional models of astrophysical objects. In class, we often used models to introduce new concepts that are less familiar than the earth and moon. For nuclear fusion, for example, balls of different colors simulated neutrons and protons that students "fused" into helium.

In addition to explicit three-dimensional models, we incorporated several kinesthetic learning activities into lectures to assist students with visualizing more complex processes and relationships. An exploration of radiation and convection in stars to transport energy from the interior to the surface used balloons to represent the energy produced by fusion. Students carried the balloons from the front to the back of the lecture hall to simulate convection whereas we batted the balloons from our seats to simulate radioactive diffusion. Following the balloon experiments, Java applets on the Web provided simulations of these phenomena in a more formal context.

We simulated the evolution of star clusters using balloons of different colors and sizes. Large blue and white balloons represented massive stars, and smaller yellow, orange, and red balloons were used for less massive stars. Students blew up the balloons to the size corresponding to their mass, and then we "evolved" the star cluster into old age. A Java applet allowed students to follow the evolution of the cluster in graphical form, and students were able to see that the massive stars quickly evolved to become supernovas and popped their balloons at the appropriate time. Less massive stars remain hydrogen burners for a much longer time.

A third kinesthetic visualization adapted from the CAT, "class modeling" (Angelo and Cross, 1993), involved the use of globular star clusters to locate the center of the Milky Way galaxy. (Globular star clusters occur throughout the galaxy but concentrate near the center.) Students were given cards identifying themselves as various types of objects found in the Milky Way, including globular clusters. Two students received cards identifying themselves as the sun and the galactic center. The "sun" and the "globular clusters" were asked to stand, and all students were then asked to locate the galactic center. The class modeling was followed with graphical and schematic depictions of the distribution of real globular clusters in the galaxy.

Visualization Through Drawing and Illustration. In addition to three-dimensional models and kinesthetic exercises, students demonstrated concepts in astronomy through drawings and illustrations. Students were asked to sketch the Milky Way galaxy (a form of the "concept map" CAT) at the beginning of class and again at the end, including as much detail as they could. The resulting drawings were analyzed to determine the level of detail included.

Figure 4.5 conveys the result that the students were able to provide significantly more detail in their sketches at the end of class than they could at the beginning. Although each of the specific items checked (for example, spiral arms, bulge, and halo) were present in a higher percentage of the students' drawings at the end of class, the most significant increases were in noting the galaxy's halo, bar, and central black hole. In addition, some students were able to add additional details, including gas, the globular clusters, the rotation of the Milky Way, and a numerical estimate of the size of the galaxy. Students were able to portray the astrophysical concepts through visual rather than verbal description, including the correct relative size and scale of the galaxy and its contents.

To continue the visualization of astronomy concepts, students were required to complete several projects, which could include an original work of art or a children's book, both illustrating any astronomy concept a student felt was important. Although some students depicted familiar scenes (the night sky, a sunset, the Milky Way), others attempted to render

Figure 4.5. Structure of the Milky Way

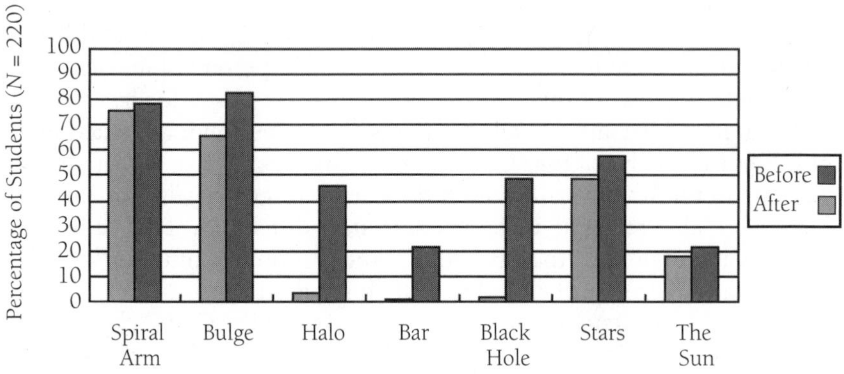

detailed concepts such as the interior structure of the sun or the interactions of binary stars through art. One student created a three-dimensional wall hanging to explain the Doppler shift of light, and another modeled the lunar surface in plaster of paris. (Examples of the students' art can be seen on the Web at http://www.indiana.edu/~flp.) Students also explained the concept depicted in their artwork in a written paragraph, the "documented problem solution" CAT (Angelo and Cross, 1993). These paragraphs revealed students' attempts to organize and structure astronomical knowledge in ways meaningful to them.

Progress But Still a Road Ahead. Throughout the course, students struggled to place unfamiliar concepts into a landscape beyond direct human experience. The use of visualization helped them to structure the concepts of astronomy, but many students had difficulty leaving the familiar world to tackle concepts beyond their own experience. Given an option, they often chose the easy way out and stayed within the conceptual framework of the familiar night sky. To encourage students to move beyond what they already know, visualization assignments should be revised to place students into more unfamiliar territory. For example, an assignment to produce a work of art could specify that the art should show a concept as seen from somewhere other than earth.

Conclusions

From these experiences in our teaching of introductory astronomy, we conclude the following:

Students learn abstract concepts more easily by beginning with concrete questions and empirical observations, rather than with fully developed theories.

Given a concrete challenge, students can successfully apply recently learned concepts to create interesting and plausible solutions.

To teach students to build complex abstract theoretical models, it is probably necessary to give them practice with feedback and guide them in specific steps.

Many students are unable to derive an understanding of abstract concepts from schematic diagrams, even when supported by explanatory text.

Students are familiar with verbal descriptions of astronomical relationships, but their understanding includes significant misconceptions about the size and scale of astronomical bodies.

Asking students to construct two- and three-dimensional models of astronomical concepts helps them develop a more complete and more correct understanding of astronomy.

Assessments are critical for evaluating strategies, gauging student progress, uncovering new dimensions of the problem, and identifying areas for future development.

Interactions with faculty in different disciplines clarify the role of discipline-specific thinking in teaching and learning and help us recognize the learning strategies that our students bring to their study of astronomy.

References

Angelo, T. A., and Cross, K. P. *Classroom Assessment Techniques: A Handbook for College Teachers.* 2nd ed. San Francisco: Jossey-Bass, 1993.

Bransford, J. D., Brown, A. L., and Cocking, R. R. *How People Learn: Brain Mind, Experience, and School.* Washington, D.C.: National Academy Press, 2000.

Ellis, A. B., Landis, C. R., and Meeker, K. "Classroom Assessment Techniques Concept Tests" [online]. n.d. Madison: University of Wisconsin. http://www.flaguide.org/cat/contests/contests1.php. Accessed June 17, 2004.

Hake, R. R. "Interactive-Engagement Versus Traditional Methods: A Six-Thousand-Student Survey of Mechanics Test Data for Introductory Physics Courses." *American Journal of Physics,* 1998, 66(1), 64–74.

Novak, G. M., Patterson, E. T., Gavrin, A. D., and Christian, W. *Just-in-Time Teaching: Blending Active Learning with Web Technology.* Upper Saddle River, N.J.: Prentice Hall, 1999.

Straits, W. J., and Wilke, R. R. "Activities-Based Astronomy: An Evaluation of an Instructor's First Attempt and Its Impact on Student Characteristics." *Astronomy Education Review,* 2003, 1(2), 46–64.

RICHARD H. DURISEN *is professor and chair of the Department of Astronomy at Indiana University.*

CATHERINE A. PILACHOWSKI *is professor of astronomy at Indiana University.*

5

To teach students particular ways of thinking in the humanities, three faculty in literature and creative writing discover how to conceptualize these approaches for students and model them or have students model them in the classroom, and they assess the results on student learning.

Decoding the Humanities

Tony Ardizzone, Fritz Breithaupt, Paul C. Gutjahr

The humanities might seem to be much less amenable to the process of decoding the disciplines than the natural sciences. The precision of the sciences makes it easier to define, model, and assess disciplinary operations. But there are specific ways of thinking implicit in each discipline in the humanities, and students who do not master these approaches are almost certainly doomed to do badly in these courses. In fact, it could be argued that the nature of these disciplines makes explicit modeling even more important because students, who are quite aware that they must learn new ways of thinking in a science course, may not even suspect that this is equally true of courses in areas such as literary analysis.

The three authors of this chapter have applied the Decoding the Disciplines model to the study of literature. Each of us has begun by identifying a crucial point in our courses where large numbers of students encounter obstacles to learning. We have then defined the kinds of mental operations that an expert in the field uses to overcome such bottlenecks. We have modeled these processes for our students and given them an opportunity to practice them on their own and to receive feedback. Finally, we have sought to systematically assess the extent to which students have mastered these mental processes.

All three of us have recognized that we faced obstacles from two directions. On the one hand, we need to encourage learners to go beyond the obvious, literal meaning of literary texts, to move beyond the "expositional mode," as Ardizzone puts it. On the other hand, learners have to develop a sense that not all products of speculation are equally valid. They have to develop criteria to distinguish between better and worse arguments or writing styles.

NEW DIRECTIONS FOR TEACHING AND LEARNING, no. 98, Summer 2004 © Wiley Periodicals, Inc.

Ardizzone, a professor of creative writing, observed that his students' writing often lacked vitality. He defined as a crucial bottleneck the difficulty his students had in going beyond mere "expositional writing" and, for this reason, created a model of poetry writing that one could call the reverse engineering of a literary text. Starting with a famous poem, he speculated how the poet *might* have begun with a more naïve, expositional piece of writing. In his modeling, he enhances the poem word by word to show the transition from expositional to poetic writings.

The students of English professor Gutjahr found it difficult to distinguish between better and worse readings of a literary text. To overcome this bottleneck, he helped them discover for themselves the seemingly cryptic code within a text. This modeling fulfills the dual task of showing the students that the code is not "made up" by the professor and that there are specific metaphorical layers within a text that one can follow.

Breithaupt, a professor of Germanic comparative literature, faced a similar bottleneck in that he wanted to help students distinguish different approaches to literary analysis and to master structural analysis. He assumed that students would be able to distinguish between different approaches if they were led through it once in a game format. This eased the anxieties connected with the bottleneck, and it involved a surprise that could reinforce learning.

All three of us gave our students an opportunity to actively practice these ways of thinking, and each devised strategies for assessing students' mastery of these operations. Each of us structured his approach to make the lesson accessible to a larger number of students.

Bridging the Writing of Exposition with Creative Writing (Ardizzone)

"Introductory Creative Writing" is a course in the fundamentals of writing poetry and fiction that enrolls approximately 110 students. In small sections, the students read, discuss, and write short analyses of a variety of model texts (poems and short stories). They also write a series of creative exercises, as well as four fully drafted poems and a fully drafted short story of at least ten pages in length. To provide the students with a viable background in these genres, I present a weekly lecture on the fundamentals of poetic and fictional craft.

After teaching the course several times, I observed that although nearly all students successfully passed the exams and completed their creative assignments on time, a significant number had difficulty with the most basic aspects of creative writing. Despite models and advice to the contrary, their writing remained expositional. These students appeared to use the same strategies they had been taught in composition in their attempts to write a poem or story. Their work was not necessarily uninteresting or weak, but it clearly lacked the vitality of well-written poetry and fiction. I concluded

Exhibit 5.1. "Morning Song" by Sylvia Plath

Love set you going like a fat gold watch.
The midwife slapped your footsoles, and your bald cry
Took its place among the elements.

Our voices echo, magnifying your arrival. New statue.
In a drafty museum, your nakedness
Shadows our safety. We stand round blankly as walls.

I'm no more your mother
Than the cloud that distills a mirror to reflect its own slow
Effacement at the wind's hand.

All night your moth-breath Flickers among the flat pink roses. I wake to listen:
A far sea moves in my ear.

One cry, and I stumble from bed, cow-heavy and floral
In my Victorian nightgown.
Your mouth opens clean as a cat's. The window square

Whitens and swallows its dull stars. And now you try
Your handful of notes;
The clear vowels rise like balloons.

Source: All lines from "Morning Song" from *Ariel* by Sylvia Plath. Copyright © 1961 by Ted Hughes.
Reprinted by permission of HarperCollins Publishers Inc.

that, despite models and advice to the contrary, these students continued to write in primarily expositional modes.

I identified this as a bottleneck and focused on strategies that could help these students bridge their current skills as fairly competent writers of exposition with their new, emerging skills as creative writers. To do so, I decided to model in lecture how a creative work might have been written. For this lesson, I chose Sylvia Plath's poem "Morning Song" as an example and included it among the assigned readings for lecture. During the lecture, I presented the poem to the class on a transparency and read it aloud (Exhibit 5.1).

I then posed the question, "How *might* Sylvia Plath have gone about writing this poem?"

I asked the class to imagine that Plath was a student in a creative writing class similar to theirs and that she had been given the following assignment: "Write a poem about someone you love and address the poem to the loved one." I told the class to imagine that Plath was taking the class shortly after she had given birth to her first child and that she chose her child as the poem's subject. I then offered them a possible opening to the poem, using sentences that the students who were writing expositionally might write themselves. Key words (ones that Plath uses in her actual poem) I put in all capitals:

You were a child of LOVE.
Ted and I both LOVED each other then.
Our love was wonderful, warm, GOLDEN.
I remember Mrs. Fiore, the MIDWIFE from downstairs,
Making you CRY. The CLOCK ticking on the hospital wall.
I remember how FAT you were, your little BALD head.

In a column on the right side of the transparency, I then gave them a prompt, one they had learned from the previous lecture, "Move from abstractions to particular images." I asked them to imagine Plath beginning the poem a second time but this time with the strategy of taking a key concept from what she had written and attempting to use it metaphorically: "Love got you started like a. . . ."

Second prompt: "Be specific and concrete. Look to the draft for help." I then offered new possible opening lines:

Love got you started like a fat gold clock.
Love set you going like a fat gold watch.

"There," I said. "There's a fine first line for a poem. So let's continue."

The midwife made you cry
Prompt: "Be specific. Appeal to the senses."
The midwife slapped your footsoles, and your naked cry

I questioned the word "naked" and offered the following:

your shrill cry
your bald cry. Filled the room.
Filled the silence of the room.
Let us know you were alive.
Took its place in the room with us.
Took its place among the elements.

I continued to model a possible writing process for the remainder of the first half of the poem, providing prompts (to be specific, to use imagery, to appeal to the senses) and allowing the students to ask questions at any step in the process.

Following the lecture, I assessed its success through a "minute paper" Classroom Assessment Technique (CAT) (Angelo and Cross, 1993). I asked the students two questions: "What did you learn most from today's lecture?" and "Are there any concepts you feel less sure about that you think require more specific explanation and further illustration?" Following a lecture in February 2004, eighty-four students completed the minute paper.

**Table 5.1. Assessing Learning Concepts for Eighty-Four
Creative Writing Students**

Concept Learned	Number of Comments on the Concept	Percentage of Total Comments
Shaping a poem through word choice	40	29%
Occasion	35	26
Using concrete images	30	22
Writing in the moment for first drafts	12	9
Using similes and metaphors	12	9
Deeper understanding of the readings	4	3
Miscellaneous	3	2

Responses to the first question helped me assess the level of their understanding. The results have been broken up into seven categories listed in order of most- to least-mentioned concepts (Table 5.1). These responses tell me that nearly all of the students say they understood the lecture's central concepts.

Responses to the second question helped me begin the subsequent lecture as well as bridge each lecture to the next. Sorting the answers led to six general categories (Table 5.2). Many students wrote positive comments explaining their confidence in the material, and fifty-nine of the eighty-four respondents had no questions. This feedback suggests that I can begin the next lecture with only a brief summary of the above material, invite specific questions, and then move on to new concepts.

Based on the students' responses and a later evaluation of their writing, I concluded that the lesson was successful in helping students understand and learn a way to bridge their expositional skills with the writing of poetry and fiction.

Table 5.2. Further Questions on Writing Process

Comments and Questions	Number of Comments	Percentage of Total Comments
No questions	59	70%
More on the concept of "occasion"	8	10
Advice on the writing process and wording	6	7
Turning the abstract to concrete	4	5
Linking occasion to simile and metaphor	4	5
Miscellaneous	2	2

Double and Triple Meanings in Literary Analysis (Gutjahr)

Often in my introductory freshman literature courses, I take a moment to have students speak about what they do not like about the study of literature. Two complaints seem to always rise to the surface. First, they are bothered by the subjective nature of the enterprise. Unlike science and mathematics, there are no "right" answers, and this bothers them. It seems to outrage their sense of justice and fair play. Second, they have become convinced somewhere along the line that the study of literature is much like the process of solving an incredibly obscure code or puzzle whose answer is known only to the teacher, who frequently takes sadistic pleasure in making them guess an author's intent or a text's true meaning.

These complaints are interesting because, on the one hand, students are complaining that they hate the fact that there is no right answer when it comes to literary analysis while, on the other hand, they are complaining that there is a hidden right answer for which they are forced into a fruitless and painful search to discover. Early in my freshman literature classes, then, I attempt to address both these complaints by leading students into an exercise that shows them that neither of these complaints is entirely valid. Literary analysis actually demands that a student take a kind of middle road between these two positions: there may not be a right answer, but there are certainly better and worse positions to argue when it comes to what a given text might mean.

This failure to understand the basic project of literary analysis is a major bottleneck to student success. The exercise I address to strike at the root of these complaints involves a closer examination of the use of metaphorical language in literary texts. In the largest course I teach—a 280-person lecture-based course centered on a historical overview of best-selling novels in the United States—I dedicate an entire lecture to modeling for my students the process of recognizing the use of symbolic language in literary texts. I begin the lecture by shying away from the literary term *metaphorical* and simply ask students to reflect for a moment on how language can have double and even triple meanings in certain contexts.

To give them an example before we even begin to look at a literary passage, I show a five-minute clip from the famous Humphrey Bogart and Lauren Bacall movie *The Big Sleep*. I have them view an interchange in which Bogart and Bacall are sitting in a bar ostensibly talking about horse racing. There are several visual and tonal clues throughout the clip, however, that the discussion is about much more than horse racing. As they banter about "staying in the saddle," "coming from behind," riding "over a distance of ground," and "coming home free," students quickly pick up that the scene is one full of flirting and sexual innuendo. On one level, Bogart and Bacall's discussion is about horse racing, but on another level, it is about the possibility of their engaging in prolonged and wild sex.

After discussing for a moment Hollywood production codes and how such language was often used in film noir to sidestep certain restrictions Hollywood motion pictures faced in the first part of the twentieth century, students began to warm to the idea that writers might indeed be using language in creative ways that convey multiple meanings. I then moved students to consider a passage from the text for the day, a seduction novel from the 1840s by George Lippard named *The Quaker City*. I had them turn to a page in their text and look specifically at the following passage, telling them to pay particular attention to the context of the quotation and the possible multiple meanings to be found in the language. The passage is short and runs as follows:

> Lorrimer advanced toward the crouching girl. He had been sure of his victim; he did not dream of any sudden outburst of terror from the half swooning maiden as she lay, helpless on his breast. As he advanced, a change came over his appearance. His face grew purple, and the veins of his eyes filled with thick blood. He trembled as he walked across the floor, and his chest heaved and throbbed beneath his white vest, as though he found it difficult to breathe.
>
> God Save poor Mary, now!
>
> Looking over her shoulder, she caught a gleam of his blood-shot eye, and read her ruin there (1995, p. 12).

To help students with this exercise, I passed out a three-by-five-inch index card to have them record their thoughts. I did not have them put anything on these cards but the possible multiple meanings they found in these lines. I then collected these cards and moved into the lecture. This learning tool is something others have called "focused listing," a process in which students list a variety of answers to a question at given points in a class discussion to help them gather their thoughts, offer avenues for further investigation and discussion, and serve as a point of evaluation for where they might be in the learning process (Angelo and Cross, 1993).

The lecture itself was a discussion of pornography and reform literature in early nineteenth-century America and how Lippard's *Quaker City* is a stunning combination of both these genres. Because Lippard positions his novel as a piece of reform literature, he is careful in how he uses various lurid details within his text. After giving a number of examples from the underground pornographic literature of the time, I moved to show how Lippard's novel functions as a classic example of a wolf in sheep's clothing. Ostensibly, the book is a diatribe against rape and pornography, and yet it uses countless pornographic conventions as a means to seek to eradicate the immoral, pornographic literature. The book promises one thing but delivers another, much like metaphorical language offers much more than a single simple message.

Near the end of the lecture, I passed out the index cards once again and had the students engage in another round of focused listing. Returning to the passage quoted above, I instructed the students to take careful note of the context (both in the text and from the history I have just given them in the lecture). I asked them to again list any multiple meanings they now see in the text based on knowledge of the flexibility of language and the historical context (Donald, 2002).

This second act of focused listing has a double benefit. I am able to see how much students have learned in the course of the lecture, but more important, it allows the students to see that they have indeed learned something in the course of the lecture. Students feel empowered by the exercise and offer comments such as "Wow! I see it now. This passage is so dirty!!" or "How about that, a reformer in need of being reformed. Who would have thought?"

In a sample of 220 students, the focused listing exercises were illuminating. At the beginning of the class, 23 students left their cards blank, 11 students doodled or wrote meaningless phrases on their cards, and 141 students recorded nothing on their cards beyond a simple description of the action—some variation of: Lorrimer had become passionate and he was going to rape Mary. Forty-five students actually went beyond summarizing the plot to make some attempt at a literary interpretation that played with the language.

In the second focused listing, multiple meanings abounded. Only two students turned in blank cards. No one doodled or turned in a card with meaningless phrases. Twenty-six students maintained a plot-summary answer, but the remaining 192 students offered extended answers on the multilayered and metaphorical meanings found in Lippard's text. While only seven students picked up on the phallic imagery in the first focused listing, the second listing showed that seventy-one students now saw that Lippard was positioning Lorrimer as a giant walking phallus, throbbing with "thick blood," "purple," and ready to attack with its single "blood-shot eye" (Figure 5.1).

The value in the exercise comes in that it helps students to see the fun of playing with the language, along with the fact that by studying historical settings and being familiar with various literary conventions, one is able to recognize more complex patterns and meanings in an author's word choice and rhetorical strategies. While they still might view literary analysis as subjective, they also gain an appreciation that it is not entirely so. There are answers for which better and worse arguments can be made, and often the puzzles or codes they so fear can actually be a great deal of fun to attempt to figure out.

Structural Analysis as Speculation (Breithaupt)

The bottleneck that confounds students in my course on literary analysis involves the daring aspect about any interpretation: it includes speculation. I want students not only to speculate as they interpret a passage but also to

Figure 5.1. Improvement in Meaning Interpretation

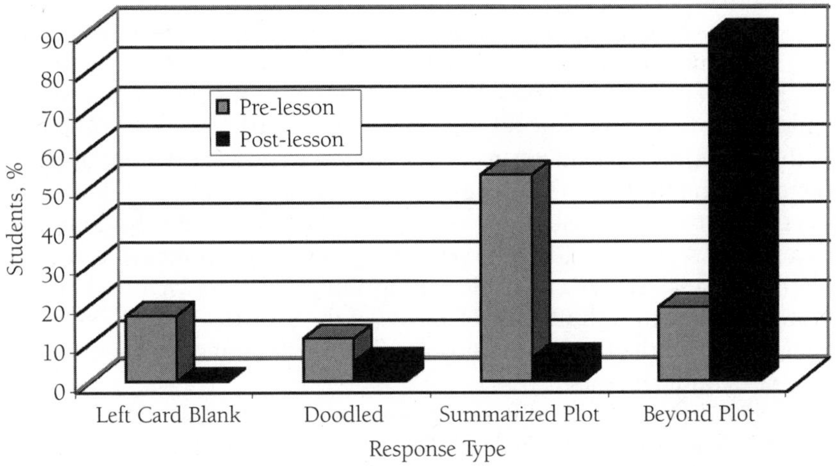

understand that some speculations are better than others. In structural analysis, one form of literary analysis, speculation is a part of analysis, not the other way round.

These issues are central to my freshman course, "A Short History of Crime: Introduction to Literary Analysis." In this course, the students typically read an excerpt from some larger text without knowing its historical context. Their task is to paint a full portrait of the culture from which the text was taken, including aspects of the culture that are not depicted in the source. I make an analogy to archeology: "You find a fragment of pottery from an extinct society; now tell me about the rituals of love of these people, their beliefs and fears, their artworks, their legal institutions, and so forth. Use all information you get from the fragment to speculate about those aspects of society that are not directly addressed in the fragment."

This is a tricky task, one that involves several subskills to get at the analysis of a culture through a text. To break it down into finer parts following step 2 in the Decoding the Disciplines model (Chapter One), I identified the key complication of this task, which is the existence of a large array of possible approaches to come to a conclusion. To produce good results, students need to be consistent with their approach. This array usually includes the following three elements (in order of increasing complexity of analysis): reshuffling of the elements of the original text, generalization of some element of the text ("everyone is like that"), and structural analysis.

Over the years, I have found that telling this to students does not enable them to do this task. When facing the task of creating different interpretations based on these three basic methods, students have significant difficulties in coming to a clear judgment. Instead of modeling it myself (step 3 in

Decoding the Disciplines), I found that the sooner the students first engaged in the task, the faster they were able to do it again. Thus, I decided to have the students model it for themselves through the following playful exercise.

The students all received the same crime text, such as a disturbing excerpt from B. E. Ellis's novel, *American Psycho*, in which a man stabs a child in the Bronx zoo (the text appears without title or author). In groups of three or four, the students were assigned to write a short story of two or three paragraphs that elaborates elements of the text, "Killing Child at Zoo," to create a love relationship. However, what the students did not know was that there were three different sets of further instructions regarding the method of analysis, given to different groups. Unbeknownst to them, the first group had to reshuffle the elements of the text, the second one had to generalize, and the third to employ a (given) structural comparison (based on a structural analysis).

Once they read their different stories to the large class, they were surprised to see the vast difference in the outcomes. In the discussion that followed, students were usually able to identify how differently they approached the basic task to continue the story by considering the three resulting stories. In fact, their characterizations of the differences tended to be more precise than when they judged similar stories that I simply posted on the blackboard. Having written a story themselves, they seemed eager to account for the different possibilities of how the same task can be solved. This task helps the students significantly to understand these three basic modes of reshuffling, generalization, and structural comparison.

I created an assessment, based loosely on the "defining features matrix" CAT (Angelo and Cross, 1993), that measures student performance before and after this exercise. In this technique, the students have to read a short crime text from a distant historical time period. Then they receive a multiple-choice questionnaire in which they have to select the most likely statements about the society, religion, love, and personality structure of the text (none of these are directly depicted in the text). Each question includes the option "there is not enough information to make such a statement." To provide fair comparisons, there is an A and a B version of the CAT. The day before the practice exercise described above, half the class took the A version and the other half the B version. On the day after the exercise, the versions were reversed.

I grouped the replies in four categories: simply wrong answers, no answer ("there is not enough information to make such a statement"), an answer based on generalization, and an answer that employs structural comparison. Student responses revealed a definite shift toward structural comparison; twice as many students made structural comparisons on the day after the exercise (Table 5.3).

What I found most telling—even more than the shift toward structural comparison—was that students usually did not feel any longer that there was "not enough information" to make assumptions about those things not explicitly stated in the text. Apparently, the exercise motivated them to make

Table 5.3. Student Responses on Assessment Questions, by Category

Category	Before Exercise, %	After Exercise, %
Wrong answer	16%	12%
"Not enough information"	21	3
Generalization	48	55
Structural comparison	14	30

an informed guess. In fact, there were still quite a lot of wrong answers in the week after the exercise, but the exercise seemed to provide students with the skill and will to speculate. Of course, this before-and-after assessment does not capture students' long-term grasp of the basic distinction. A much longer testing sequence would be required to demonstrate this.

I would like to close by reflecting about the pros and cons of the structural comparisons practice exercise. The basic approach here is designed for those situations in which the method of student work is an explicit topic of discussion in class ("how" questions). The main advantage of the exercise is that it provides students with firsthand experience of solving the task. They "do it" without fully being aware of it. This is both encouraging and empowering for students. The different results usually serve as clear and memorable reference points for students who struggle to keep the methods apart. The group work and creative writing aspect usually work well with all students, and they comment about the "fun" they had. The exercise is time-intensive and has a limited range of uses, namely, to compare and contrast different theoretical approaches. At the same time, it could be used with little adaptation for scientific techniques as well. The fact that students do not know that they have different sets of instructions creates a beautiful riddle for them.

Conclusion

What becomes visible in our three exercises is the difference between a mere "example" and "modeling." In the case of how to solve a task, the professor forgoes the moment of crisis that students face when left alone with a task. However, by these modeling activities, students experience their professor in an active moment of investigating. In all our exercises, the students observe that their professor actually makes choices instead of merely presenting a solution.

References

Angelo, T. A., and Cross, K. P. *Classroom Assessment Techniques: A Handbook for College Teachers.* 2nd ed. San Francisco: Jossey-Bass, 1993.

Chandler, R., *The Big Sleep* [film]. (Hawks, H., director). United States: MGM/UA Home Entertainment Inc., 1946.

Donald, J. *Learning to Think: Disciplinary Perspectives*. San Francisco: Jossey-Bass, 2002.

Ellis, B. E. *American Psycho*. New York: Simon & Schuster, 1991.

Lippard, G. *The Quaker City: or, The Monks of Monk Hall*. Originally published in the 1840s. Amherst: University of Massachusetts Press, 1995 (reprint).

TONY ARDIZZONE *is professor of English and director of the Creative Writing Department at Indiana University.*

PAUL C. GUTJAHR *is associate professor of English, American Studies, and Religious Studies at Indiana University.*

FRITZ BREITHAUPT *is professor of Germanic Studies at Indiana University.*

6

To think like a historian, students must select and assess evidence that supports interpretations of the meaning of the past. Three historians focus on aspects of this task and pursue different approaches to teach their students to use evidence.

Learning to Use Evidence in the Study of History

Valerie Grim, David Pace, Leah Shopkow

While students tend to see history as a body of facts to be memorized, historians see their field as a body of narratives presenting carefully selected and assessed evidence that supports interpretations of the meaning of the past. Our goal as historians is to teach our undergraduate students to create such narratives for themselves, but this is difficult without a systematic reevaluation of how we teach them. The Decoding the Disciplines process has provided each of us with a framework for rethinking how we teach students about the use of evidence and other crucial skills. We began by defining crucial bottlenecks to learning. Then we explored the kinds of thinking that professional historians do at those points and modeled them for our students. After giving students an opportunity to practice these skills and receive feedback, we assessed how well they learned these basic operations. The results of this process have been encouraging.

Historians are notorious for disagreeing with each other about nearly everything. Thus, it is significant that we three historians independently chose to focus on the same bottleneck. We each decided that the difficulty students have with identifying and deploying evidence in history courses was such an obstacle to their learning that it deserved systematic attention.

Using evidence in the study of history is different from what many other academic disciplines expect of undergraduates. In the sciences, for example, students may not enter the realm of uncertainty and debate about the foundations of knowledge until they reach the graduate level. In introductory history courses, however, they are sometimes asked on the first day of class to weigh evidence supporting the relative merits of different interpretations.

Students who do not understand how historians use evidence are almost certain to fail at the core tasks in this discipline.

In the absence of clear ideas of how to treat evidence, beginning history students may make generalizations with no evidence at all. They may be unable to identify pertinent evidence and consequently write down all they know in no clear order. More sophisticated students may use relevant evidence but not make explicit how this information supports their theses. In other words, uninitiated students are like three sorts of inept defense attorneys: the first produces broad statements about a client's innocence without any proof, the second presents details without linking them to broader arguments about innocence, and the third produces both evidence and theories of innocence but fails to link the one to the other (Pace and Pugh, 1995).

All three historians required students to gather evidence, select pertinent evidence, and use evidence in arguments. However, we have taken the historian's prerogative to disagree with each other as to what part of the problem to focus on and what interventions to pursue in the solution thereof. Shopkow selected the simple identification of potential evidence in primary sources as the bottleneck she wanted to work on. She had her students choose a category of inquiry and then list all the evidence available in one primary source that might have bearing on that category. Grim's bottleneck focused on disciplining the students' historical imaginations through the selection and application of appropriate evidence so that they might understand the past historically but without losing the human empathy understood to be essential to the historian's craft. Her students engaged in a series of role-playing assignments in which they were required to use historical evidence to shape a hypothetical historical persona. Pace concentrated on the bottleneck of getting students to support their arguments with evidence. In his series of assignments, students were asked to use evidence in increasingly sophisticated ways.

In the sections of the article that follow, we each describe our projects and findings. In our conclusion, we reflect on the implications of our collective findings and suggest further steps we might take to help our students succeed at the skills central to the historical discipline.

Recognizing Evidence as Evidence (Shopkow)

Before students can use evidence from primary sources in support of arguments, they must recognize evidence when they see it. But students are often unsure what they are supposed to get out of primary sources when they read them. Therefore, in my junior-level class on the early Middle Ages in Europe (200–1100 CE), I decided to focus on getting students to recognize potential evidence in primary sources, even if they were unsure how that evidence might be used.

Because evidence is always relational—that is, it is evidence for a thesis, about a phenomenon, or concerning an event—I began by encouraging the students to think of sorting potential evidence into categories. I gave them a hypertext version of a passage from Roland Barthes's *S/Z* (1974), where Barthes uses five categories (or "codes") into which he sorts the contents of a short story by Balzac. (The students were unclear as to how Barthes chose these categories, so the example was not helpful. In future classes, I will use a group exercise instead, in which the class itself chooses the categories.)

Next I had the students read *The Passions of Saints Perpetua and Felicity*, an early-third-century text, and asked them to collect all the potential evidence they could find on a topic that struck their interest—for example, the family, the Roman state, women, the Christian community. They were also to ask an historical question about their collected evidence and to decide whether they had enough evidence to answer it. ("Historical questions" deal with the nature of particular times and places or about change over time.) Students collected an average of 16.5 pieces of evidence, with a range from 4 to 35.

At the end of the semester, the class returned to the problem of recognizing potential evidence. The students were about to write their final papers, which they would need to illustrate with abundant primary source evidence from the *Book of Sainte Foy*, a collection of miracle stories from eleventh-century southern France (Sheingorn, 2003). The last assignment before the final paper mimicked the first assignment the students had done: they had to choose a topic for their paper and collect all the potential evidence they found that pertained to that topic from the *Book of Sainte Foy*. The students were once again asked to pose an historical question based on the evidence they had collected, but this time they were also required to provide a tentative answer (it was pointed out to them that their answer was actually a thesis about their evidence). Although the students were permitted to change their theses in the final version of the paper, they were expected to write on the topic they had chosen, for which they had already collected the evidence.

For the second assignment, most of the students collected many more pieces of evidence than they had for the first short assignment. They identified on average 32.7 pieces of evidence, with a range of 1 (obviously a student who had blown off the assignment) to 103. The question here was whether simply gathering a lot of potential evidence would lead the students to use more evidence in their papers and, if they did so, whether their papers were better for it.

Indeed, collecting more evidence did, in most cases, mean students used more evidence in their papers (with a correlation of $R = 0.49$). Evidence in the papers was counted by the number of citations each student made as all evidence required separate citations. Student papers contained, on average, 18.9 citations. There was also a good correlation ($R = 0.46$) between the number of citations made by a student and the student's grade on the paper. Students who received a grade in the A range averaged 25.5

citations, students in the B range averaged 21.9 citations, and students in the C range or lower averaged only 15 citations.

The abundance of citations, however, was not the whole story. One student paper had twenty-one citations but received a grade of C; this student made many factual errors, misread the text in many places, included irrelevant information, and contradicted himself. Another student who used only four citations received a grade of B+; this student focused on four specific anecdotes from the collection of miracles and provided an in-depth analysis of each, with one citation per anecdote. In the middle category was a student whose B paper contained forty-nine citations. I found this paper somewhat unfocused, and the student had some writing difficulties that contributed to this grade. But generally speaking, the more evidence a student considered, as indicated by the number of citations, the stronger the paper tended to be.

Using Evidence to Shape the Historical Imagination (Grim)

During my fourteen years' experience teaching history, I have found it increasingly difficult to get students to use specific details to answer questions or to support a position they are taking on an issue. To be successful in this course, students needed to be able to situate a personal viewpoint within a critical framework. To help students achieve this objective in my freshman-level African American history class of 110 students, I designed an assignment that involved historical imagination. So that students might develop critical consciousness, I asked them to imagine that they lived in another period, envisioning themselves as someone living and feeling the emotions of people in the past as they explained developments during a historical period.

The basic learning task in this creative role-play exercise required students to think in historical context. In ten assignments across five weeks, students could assume the identity of such persons as editors, advertisers, letter writers, journalists, teachers, preachers, politicians, lawyers, diary keepers, playwrights, artists, composers, and musicians, telling the story of black people through different media. Modeling the exercise for students, I became an American Revolutionary War soldier, describing the broader historical times as well as how developments during this time affected me personally. This example provided a few guidelines for students' work. The students had to synthesize by using details in a personalized manner to show how they comprehended and analyzed developments, and they had to integrate specific evidence with the given historical contexts.

Students were given occasions to practice the skills involved in the creative role-play exercise. They were asked to summarize and discuss a current event to show they understood content and comprehended the issues.

They also were asked to engage in role-play using current events to form historical contexts and critiques. In addition, students received written feedback concerning how to assume identity.

Although I provided comments on student exercises, after three assignments most students were not grasping how to connect the personal and general to broader historical developments through specific analysis. In fact, some students struggled to give details or synthesize these components, and very few of the role-play activities showed a deep understanding of the period. The majority simply offered personal reactions, like that of the student who wrote, "We will not back down in times of difficulty, and we will not apologize for what we have to say to this nation. We are who we are. We do say these things in a condemning voice; we say it loud and proud so that we will be heard." Most students could express emotional and personal responses, even though they failed to show balanced reasoning that connected the personal to the broader historical context that worked as a form of critique.

Because students were struggling to complete the role-play weekly assignments according to instructions, I created an in-class assignment to practice the process. This time I had students compose a letter home that was to begin with a broad summary of happenings in Bloomington. This letter was to be specific and personal by discussing some of the events and developments at Indiana University, and it had to become critical, raising questions and contextualizing experiences within the larger community and campus cultures. The letters were read aloud in class, and students were asked to comment on which letters satisfied the criteria and why. Students were then instructed to use this format to complete the remaining three assignments.

To examine the effectiveness of the in-class assignment in helping students achieve the learning objective, I compared students' performance on assignment number 5 (the assignment before the in-class letter), the in-class letter itself, and two assignments made after the letter (assignments 8 and 10). Most students were more successful in the exercises done after the in-class letter, although the performance of a significant minority remained the same (see Figure 6.1 for scores). Only for a small percentage of students did performance levels go down, and the performance of almost half went up (Figure 6.2). One student's response to a reading concerning the reformer and statesman Marcus Garvey reflects the kind of growth that eventually emerged in these assignments: "Garvey states that his organization is set up not to hate people, but to better the condition of black people everywhere in the world. The conditions of black people in different locations throughout the world are so different, and I believe that it will be very hard to unify black people from America and Africa. That would be like finding a way to unite white people of British descent with people from the Soviet Union."

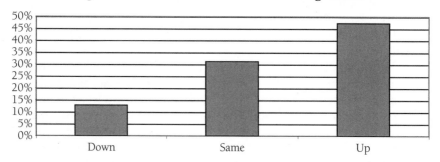

Figure 6.1. Scores on Selected Assignments

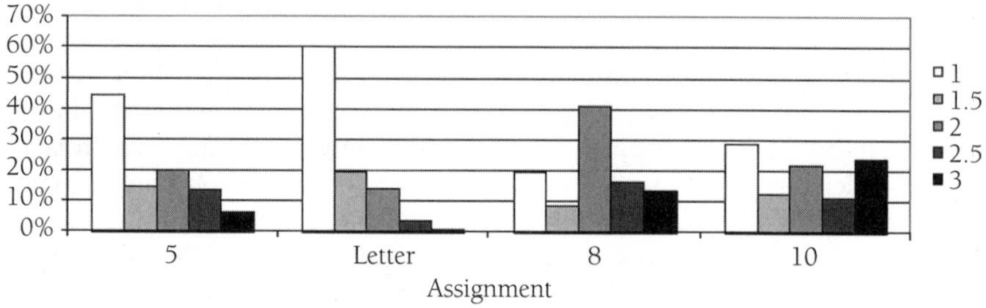

Figure 6.2. Student Success Across Assignments

Selecting and Deploying Evidence in Historical Arguments (Pace)

It is embarrassing to admit that I wrote "Evidence?" on papers for almost two decades before I systematically explained to students precisely how they were supposed to use evidence in a history course. Recognizing that historians support their arguments differently from experts in the other disciplines my students were studying, I realized that I had to define the specific steps that historians perform to make an interpretation credible. My analysis of student errors suggested three steps were necessary. To reason historically, students had to, first, recognize what kinds of evidence would be required to support a particular interpretation; second, search the materials assigned in the course for evidence that matched these criteria; and third, make explicit for the reader the reasons why each piece of evidence made the argument more convincing.

The next step was to find ways to model these skills. In the first class of a course on the history of the future, I compared an historical argument with a story in which the introduction of relevant details made the account more convincing. I introduced them to the metaphor of the three attorneys (described earlier), took them through several passages from secondary sources assigned in the course, and discussed the ways evidence was used to support an interpretation.

It was clear that students would need regular opportunities to practice this skill and receive feedback on the process. I therefore included tasks on the use of evidence in the weekly Web assignments and in-class team exercises. I began with simple questions that depended largely on recall. In the second week, I asked them to identify three bits of evidence that a historian was using to support his position in a particular passage. In the next stage, they were asked to generate mini-interpretations and to find evidence that would support them.

This pattern was repeated several times over the next several weeks of the course, as students were asked to identify residues of the Christian Apocalypse in secular visions of the end of the world, to specify the assumptions about human beings in nineteenth-century technological utopias, and to provide similarities and differences in the values and assumptions of two very different authors. In each case, the students were asked not only to answer the question but also to provide specific evidence and to explain what it was about that evidence that lent credence to their answer.

I also began to add exercises that more fully represented the way that historians pose and answer questions. For example, I presented them with a general statement that made a strong claim concerning the strength of the continuities between eighteenth- and nineteenth-century visions of progress and asked them to find passages in the readings that either supported or undercut this position. This not only reinforced the notion that history is about supporting interpretations, it also gave students practice at responding to one of the standard forms of essay questions in the discipline. This pattern was repeated in other exercises that required them to define the thesis in a secondary source, to point to evidence that was being used to support the thesis, and finally to explain the nature of that support.

To evaluate changes across the semester in the students' understanding of how to deploy evidence, I gave a random set of the students a "pretest" at the beginning of the semester. They were asked to read a standard history essay question concerning material that was not covered in my course and to indicate which of several pieces of evidence would be most appropriate to support the thesis built into the question. When I gave the same question to a different subset of my students near the end of the semester, the number of right answers had increased almost 13 percent (from 79 percent to 92 percent).

It was also useful to assess individual progress across the semester. For example, in the first two weeks, one student had difficulty with basic ways of thinking historically. He could not determine what was relevant, and he could not distinguish the rhetorical framework and the author's interpretations from historical facts. By the third week, he was able to identify examples of evidence being used to support the author's argument, but given a thesis only, he still had difficulty identifying the evidence that would support it. In the assignment for week four, the same student had no difficulty finding evidence to support a given thesis.

Conclusions

Because history is a forensic discipline, it makes sense that all three of us selected the proper use of evidence as both a major problem for students and an essential skill. The bottlenecks of using evidence exist because students usually come into history classes from their high school training ill prepared to think like historians: they see themselves as performers of existing stories or, worse, as repeaters of "facts." In beginning students' eyes, what makes someone a good history student is the ability to know all the relevant details of the past. They do not yet see themselves as "attorneys" who must find both the evidence and the arguments to defend their "clients" in a convincing way. That history is constructed from and based in evidence is something they have to learn.

Our three projects had different strengths. Shopkow focused students on the collection of evidence; they were the legal detectives sifting through texts for evidence and putting it in the evidence box for later use. Her project split into two tasks that experts perform simultaneously: gathering evidence and deploying it. By the end of her course, students had learned to provide the fullness of evidence needed for good historical work. Pace's project repeatedly modeled and analyzed what historians do, so that students became much better at assembling evidence to produce compelling arguments. Grim's exercises pushed her passionate advocates to uncover human motivations that connect historical struggle to agency. By her final assignment, more students understood how to use specific details and how to relate them to broader analytical contexts. Of all of us, she most fully put into practice the need for frequent practice and feedback as she graded 1,100 student papers across the semester.

But we have some joint conclusions as well. First, it is clear that although the students we get at Indiana University are, for the most part, not adequately prepared to succeed within the discipline of history, they can catch up when they are active participants in the process, when tasks are broken down for them in the right way, and when they are given regular opportunities to practice what they have learned. Our second conclusion, while obvious, is essential: as we asked our students to do the kind of focused and intense work that produces results, we had to do focused and intense work ourselves; as we asked them to do more, we also had to do more. Decoding the discipline of history is a labor-intensive process for all the parties concerned. Still, it is a process that is rich in rewards for both students and teachers.

References

Barthes, R. *S/Z*. (R. Miller, trans.). New York: Hill & Wang, 1974.
Medieval Sourcebook: St. Perpetua: "The Passion of Saints Perpetua and Felicity 203." New York: Fordham University. http://www.fordham.edu/halsall/source/perpetua.html. Accessed June 17, 2004.

Pace, D., and Pugh, S. L. *Studying for History*. New York: Harper-Collins College
Publishers, 1995.
Sheingorn, P. (trans.). *The Book of Sainte Foy*. Philadelphia: Philadelphia University
Press, 2003.

*VALERIE GRIM is interim chair and associate professor of African American and
African Diaspora Studies at Indiana University.*

*DAVID PACE is associate professor of history and codirector of the Faculty
Learning Community at Indiana University. He is also a fellow of the Carnegie
Academy for the Scholarship of Teaching and Learning.*

*LEAH SHOPKOW is director of undergraduate studies and associate professor in
the History Department at Indiana University.*

7

Two faculty in business and public and environmental affairs find that students need to move between personal-based experience, data, and a higher level of analytical reasoning. Their teaching of marketing and statistics is shown to benefit from the structured analysis and detailed assessments of the Decoding the Disciplines model.

Decoding Applied Data in Professional Schools

Barry M. Rubin, Shanker Krishnan

The two perspectives adopted in this article approach similar problems. Both of us teach courses in professional schools where the focus is on developing a conceptual understanding of various methods and then applying that understanding to address real-world problems. Both applications involve overcoming bottlenecks caused by students' misconceptions stemming from an overreliance on their own experience. In the case of marketing, students do not know how to reverse perspective and replace their own experience with marketing strategies that influence consumer decision making. With respect to introductory statistics, students have great difficulty in adding the concept of a sampling distribution to the more tangible and experience-based concept of a frequency distribution of raw data. Both learning environments involve a conceptual leap to a higher level of analytical thinking. This development is not a linear learning process. Instead, it is necessary to move back and forth between concepts and applications, such that one continually reinforces the other. In the next sections, we develop the specific applications within our disciplines using the Decoding the Disciplines model (see Chapter One).

Learning to Apply Marketing Strategy (Krishnan)

Marketing students rely on information about consumers to make decisions regarding their products. For example, pricing, advertising, channels, and product decisions hinge on an accurate understanding of consumers and their decision processes. It is not surprising that consumer decision making is a central part of the marketing strategy course. Although students generally understand how consumers make decisions, they are not able to reverse perspective and think like marketing managers. In particular, the bottleneck students face is that they do not know how to use information about consumer decision making to design actions that would influence those decisions. They rely instead on their own experience as consumers, which although relevant, may also be filled with misconceptions (Savion, 2003; Krishnan and Porter, 1998). Knowing that a particular group of consumers makes decisions in a particular manner should help identify an advertising communications strategy for this group of consumers.

According to the Decoding the Disciplines model, step 2 (Chapter One) involves a definition of how an expert would accomplish this task. In this marketing context, the steps involved in adopting a reverse perspective are as follows. Students have to:

Identify the set of attributes consumers use to make decisions about a product

Describe the weights consumers assign to these attributes based on their underlying purchase motivations

Translate how differences in motivation lead to the formation of decision rules

Understand how to group consumers into different segments based on decision rules

Identify the possible range of actions that could influence consumer decision rules

Match specific actions with the types of decision rules used by consumer segments

Consumer Decision Application. To enable students to learn how to reverse perspective, I showed them an example of a consumer decision task. Two volunteers were asked to place themselves in a scenario where they are purchasing a car. They were provided information about three car models and asked to use the information to make a selection. The class observed several aspects of the decision rules and processes, including the information requested, the sequence of information, and the amount of information. I provided a running commentary of how the students' decision making can be analyzed to understand their priorities and decision rules. I also related to the larger goals of understanding consumer, product, and context variables that might influence decision making. Finally, to help them reverse perspective, I asked the class to think about how they would market the car differently to the two student volunteers. In essence, this helped the students learn through watching the instructor model the tasks (step 3 in the model).

According to the Decoding the Disciplines model, practice in performing these steps is essential to student mastery (step 4). I created an occasion for students to practice the steps and receive feedback on how they can reverse perspectives. In the last fifteen minutes of the class session, student teams worked on a decision-making problem that necessitated that they switch perspective from consumer to marketing manager. The product was different from the example that was used earlier in class, and the students were provided data on various decision styles. Students needed to complete an analysis of the choices made by consumers using different decision rules. Further, students had to reverse perspective and identify the actions that a marketing manager could engage in to influence these consumers' decisions. (See http://www.indiana.edu/~flp for examples of materials used in these exercises.)

Results. To assess how well this system was working, I developed an assessment plan. First, I assessed students' ability to use a marketing framework to understand how consumers make the purchase decision and switch perspective from consumer to marketer. To assess their skill at this task before the targeted lesson, I asked students ($N = 42$) at the beginning of class to individually answer several questions using the Classroom Assessment Technique (CAT) called "background knowledge probe" (Angelo and Cross, 1993). Results showed that although thirty-five students (83 percent) were able to analyze their own motivations, only ten (24 percent) were able to identify other consumer motivations, and only six (14 percent) were able to reverse perspective and think about the marketing implications. During class, the modeling and corresponding discussion were framed to help students learn how to think about the marketing implications. At the end of class, students individually completed a worksheet (see Web site http://www.indiana.edu/~flp) involving consumer data on which they had to compute what different types of toothpaste consumers will choose. This worksheet also required them to show their work and provide a rationale, a form of Angelo and Cross's "documented problem solution" CAT. Analysis of results from the worksheet was encouraging. Twenty-four students (57 percent) were able to identify alternative consumer motivations, and fifteen (37 percent) were able to reverse perspective and provide marketing recommendations.

Learning to Apply Statistical Analysis (Rubin)

In both the private and public sectors, the use of statistical analysis is growing at a remarkable rate because of increased competition, globalization, and an emphasis on cost-effective processes and service delivery. Coupled with societal need and the ease of access to analytical capabilities is the intent of most universities and colleges that students in key liberal arts areas and almost all professional schools understand how to apply statistics (Kugler, Hagen, and Singer, 2003). Yet, required courses in statistical analysis are generally unsuccessful in conveying the necessary concepts for students to apply or understand statistics (Gardner and Hudson, 1999).

Bottleneck. There are a number of bottlenecks to the average student's learning or long-term retention of critical concepts in introductory statistics.

These are due to the unfamiliar nature of statistical concepts and the need to stack multiple levels of abstract thought one upon another to achieve critical insights and understanding. The sampling distribution is the leading bottleneck in the teaching and learning of statistical analysis because of its importance and students' difficulty in understanding.

Sampling distributions are a key concept in statistics but a highly problematic one for students. A sampling distribution can be defined as the relative frequency distribution of a statistic, such as the sample mean, calculated from repeated random samples of a consistent size taken from the same population. Thus, it is a distribution of the values of a statistic rather than the values of the cases that make up the raw data.

In an effort to develop an intuitive understanding of this concept among my students, I developed an exercise in which the students derive an empirical sampling distribution for the sample mean for class height by repeatedly calculating a statistic (the sample mean) from twelve random samples, each drawn independently from the class. A sample size of five was used for each sample, and each student who was selected for the sample was asked to call out his or her height in inches. After all twelve sample means were calculated, the group plotted these sample means on a frequency distribution. Students were paired for discussion purposes and to enhance the accuracy of data entry and calculation. (The exercise handout is provided at the Web site http://www.indiana.edu/~flp.)

Assessment. Just before handing out the exercise, I asked students to define and describe a sampling distribution in their own words on a three-by-five-inch index card. This is a combination of the "minute paper" and "directed paraphrasing" CATs (Angelo and Cross, 1993). The week following the exercise, the students were again asked to define this concept on an index card. I then evaluated their responses to identify the number of students who understood the concept, as indicated by their definition and descriptions.

Results for the Sampling Distribution Exercise. The first time I used this exercise, I did not tell students that they would be doing a second evaluation but instead "surprised" them with this task a week after the exercise was conducted. Twenty-six percent of the students ($N = 38$; 10 students) demonstrated sufficient understanding of the sampling distribution concept before the exercise whereas only 32 percent (12 students) demonstrated this depth of understanding after the exercise, representing an increase of only two students. This result was disappointing, and I endeavored to determine why. After discussing the outcome with several students, I realized that I needed to summarize the results of the exercise after its completion to reinforce the sampling distribution concept. Also, to emphasize the importance of understanding the outcome and concepts illustrated by the exercise, it was necessary to inform the students about the follow-up evaluation.

With these changes, this exercise has indeed proved effective in developing student understanding in my classes. The second ($N = 56$) and third times ($N = 52$) I conducted the exercise, about 28 percent of the students demonstrated sufficient understanding of the sampling distribution concept before the exercise. This percentage rose to about 68 percent following the exercise.

A qualitative comparison of the results before and after the definitions also revealed an enhancement in learning following the exercise and showed that even students who had a reasonable grasp of the concept before the exercise often improved their understanding.

Digitized Video Interviews as Motivational Aids. Another aspect of my intervention strategy for teaching introductory statistics, step 5 of the Decoding the Disciplines model, considers the motivational aspects of student learning. By addressing real problems in contextual form and linking the classroom experience with a student's future profession, I intended to motivate students to spend the time and energy needed to learn the critical concepts and analytical techniques necessary to become proficient with statistics.

I created video case studies of statistical analyses conducted by alumni who had sat in the same class as current students. By providing digitized video interviews of these former students presenting a problem and the results of their analysis, statistics can thus "come alive." These videos served as the focus of small group discussions and as active learning exercises.

To implement this technique, I showed the first half of the video to student groups and then challenged them to design the statistical procedures to solve the case. Each group's suggested procedures were discussed with the entire class. The portion of the video that described the actual solution was then viewed, followed by full-class discussion of student solutions versus the actual solution. The final component of the exercise was my summary and reinforcement of the results with respect to the use of multivariate regression analysis and its utility in an applied setting. Digitizing these videos and putting them on the Web enabled the student groups to also work on the case study outside of class.

Results for the Digitized Video Interview and Case Study. The learning outcome of this digitized video exercise first became apparent in the full-class discussion before the students saw the second half of the video. Even though none of the individual groups came up with the actual solution used, the class collectively touched on all the major elements incorporated into the regression analysis. This was surprising because I did not expect the students to be able to articulate the logic behind the outcome until the second half of the video was shown. I now believe that this was an indication of the effects that a truly motivational exercise can have on stimulating students' critical thinking and interaction through the small-group process.

The motivational and learning outcomes of this digitized video exercise were formally evaluated using a survey that I gave to the students during the class meeting immediately following the exercise. Responses to a background question indicated that the average student was unafraid of math but tended to find it boring. According to the survey responses to Likert-scale items, the large majority of students found the video helpful in understanding how regression and general statistical analysis can be applied to real-world problems. Students thought that the small-group and full-class discussions were critical to their understanding of how statistical analysis can be applied. Overall, the survey results affirmed the efficacy of the digitized video case study as the focus of a group exercise to enhance motivation and improve student learning. Moreover, the unexpected outcome that students articulated the logic of the statistical technique in the middle of the exercise further supports the finding that this case study technique is a successful active and collaborative learning method.

Conclusion

Even though these two applications of new teaching and learning techniques come from different disciplines, there are significant environmental contexts, commonalities of approach, and general outcomes that are shared by both instructors. First, both attempts at enhancing student learning produced a significant increase in the percentage of students who achieved mastery of the concept, and in the case of the statistics video, it also enhanced student motivation.

Second, both the marketing and statistics applications benefited from the use of CATs (Angelo and Cross, 1993) or similar explicit evaluation instruments to generate quantifiable results, rather than relying exclusively on our impressions. With the "before" and "after" evaluations, we identified the extent of student learning in both the marketing and statistical analysis contexts.

Third, we both realized the need to reinforce the major concepts addressed by the exercises immediately after their completion by summarizing and reviewing the outcome of the exercise and directly relating that outcome back to critical concepts.

Fourth, we both worked iteratively toward a successful implementation of these new teaching and learning methods. Just as our students learn from these exercises, so do we; but our learning is focused on how to better achieve the desired outcome for the exercise. It was not until the second or third attempt at implementing the marketing and sampling distribution exercises that we saw clear improvement in student learning. Instructors must be willing to experiment with these learning methods, recognizing that it will often take time and multiple iterations to develop a successful exercise.

Finally, our collective experiences support the use of the Decoding the Disciplines model, with the identification of specific bottlenecks key to designing effective learning interventions. Furthermore, both approaches created occasions for students to practice the steps and receive feedback, and we used assessment tools tailored to obtain evidence of student mastery. The final step in the model is sharing what we have learned, which is the purpose of this article.

References

Angelo, T. A., and Cross, K. P. *Classroom Assessment Techniques: A Handbook for College Teachers*. 2nd ed. San Francisco: Jossey-Bass, 1993.

Gardner, P., and Hudson, I. "University Students' Ability to Apply Statistical Procedures." *Journal of Statistics Education*, 1999, 7(1). http://www.amstat.org/ publications/jse/ secure/v7n1/gardner.cfm. Retrieved Aug. 30, 2004.

Krishnan, H. S., and Porter, T. W. "A Process Approach for Developing Skills in a Consumer Behavior Course." *Journal of Marketing Education*, 1998, 20(1), 24–34.

Kugler, C., Hagen, J., and Singer, F. "Teaching Statistical Thinking." *Journal of College Science Teaching*, 2003, 32(7), 434–439.

Magel, R. "Using Cooperative Learning in a Large Introductory Statistics Class." *Journal of Statistics Education*, 1998, 6(3). http://www.amstat.org/publications/jse/v6n3/ magel.html. Retrieved Aug. 30, 2004.

Savion, L. "Pet Theories and Naïve Misconceptions: What Students Bring to Class." *Successful Professor*, 2003, 1(4), 4–6.

BARRY M. RUBIN *is professor in the School of Public and Environmental Affairs at Indiana University.*

SHANKER KRISHNAN *is associate professor of marketing at the Kelley School of Business, Indiana University.*

8

This chapter addresses the logistical considerations for the use of collaborative learning in the Decoding the Disciplines model and presents twelve principles for successfully using teamwork in the classroom and several assessments of the efficacy of the group process.

Using Collaborative Learning Teams to Decode Disciplines: Physiology and History

Whitney M. Schlegel, David Pace

The attempt to systematically introduce students to the ways of thinking in a discipline (see Chapter One) does not stand apart from or even in opposition to other strategies that have been developed to increase student learning. In most cases, the effort to give students practice in basic disciplinary operations, step 4 of the Decoding the Disciplines model, requires applying active and collaborative strategies, whose value is widely recognized (Bosworth and Hamilton, 1994; Cooper and Robinson, 1998; Heller, Keith, and Anderson, 1992; Johnson and Johnson, 1999; Millis and Cottell, 1998; Michaelsen, 1992; Slavin, 1995; Springer, Stanne, and Donovan, 1999). The Decoding the Disciplines approach can make these techniques even more successful: the process of defining as precisely as possible what students need to be able to do to succeed in a discipline can make it easier to devise exercises that create a fruitful occasion for students to work collaboratively. In this chapter, we explore how student teams have been employed in history and physiology classrooms to engage students with disciplinary process and content, and we provide evidence that the Decoding the Disciplines model can serve to guide teaching practice in the future. The first section, by Pace, lays out the principles we have derived for successfully using collaborative learning in the classroom (see Exhibit 8.1). In the second section, Schlegel describes her rationale for including collaborative groups in her course and her strategies for assessing their effectiveness.

NEW DIRECTIONS FOR TEACHING AND LEARNING, no. 98, Summer 2004 © Wiley Periodicals, Inc.

Exhibit 8.1. Ten Principles for the Effective Use of Learning Teams

1. Conceptualize each team exercise in terms of a clear learning goal (in our case, one or more of the basic operations of the discipline).
2. Begin collaborative activities on the first day to shape student expectations.
3. Generate teams of four to five students, taking into consideration the makeup of the class. (As we have seen, the process of assigning groups can be random or purposeful so as to maximize heterogeneity.)
4. Have groups sit together in class to maximize group cohesion and overcome the anonymity of large classes.
5. Explain to the class why collaborative tools are being used in the course.
6. Send the message that teamwork is an important part of the course by making it a part of student assessment and grading.
7. Assess student reactions to team work.
8. Use group work regularly and employ both substantial and brief exercises.
9. Provide clear instructions and feedback, preferably in writing, for all team exercises.
10. Regularly have groups share with the entire class what they have been doing.
11. Assess individual student learning of skills practiced in teams.
12. Regard your students as emerging scholars. Your role is to share and facilitate their development.

Using Teams to Decode the Disciplinary Practices of Historians (Pace)

In this section, I discuss my efforts to use collaborative learning to provide students with practice and feedback in basic disciplinary operations, step 4 in the Decoding the Disciplines model. I do this in a particular ecology of learning—an upper-level history class on the culture of Paris and Berlin in the 1920s. This course has no prerequisites, nor is it a requirement for any program, and the 100 to 120 students that it attracts are from all classes and divisions of the university. In a recent semester, for example, the class of about 150 students included 29 history majors, 33 majors in other humanities disciplines, 32 from the professional schools, and 16 majors in science or math. In short, the class is a microcosm of the large modern university and a miniature Tower of Babel, in which at least twenty distinct disciplinary languages are represented.

In such a situation, there is a great temptation to teach to those students who begin the semester well grounded in the kinds of thinking required in the course and already interested in the subject matter and to leave the rest of the class to their own devices. The Decoding the Disciplines approach allowed me to escape this pedagogical cul-de-sac by systematically introducing all of my students to the basic processes of operating as a historian. I began by identifying places where the learning of many students was blocked. I then defined for myself the steps that a professional historian would take to get past this bottleneck.

One of the most important of such bottlenecks occurred whenever I asked students to analyze a text or image in preparation for placing it in its historical context. Many of the students had no idea how to begin this process. Through introspection and interviews with other historians, I realized that my students had to make explicit the assumptions and values implicit within specific cultural artifacts, such as paintings or books. Furthermore, to do so they had to begin by comparing individual works with other works from different eras and different movements in the same era. Having identified what my students had to learn how to do, I modeled these activities, gave my students an opportunity to practice them and get feedback, and devised a means of assessing whether these skills were being mastered.

Collaborative learning exercises played a crucial role in this strategy by providing opportunities for students to practice these ways of analyzing the assumptions and values underlying cultural artifacts (step 4 in the Decoding the Disciplines model; see Chapter One) and by requiring them to articulate to their teammates the steps that they were taking. In the first class I showed the students a series of double slides that contrasted images of traditional western art with avant-garde images from the 1920s. In ad hoc teams, the students compared the differences between the two sets of images, thereby reinforcing both the process of defining works through contrasts with others and the process of learning collaboratively.

This kind of informal ad hoc group work, however, has its limitations. Students do not have a chance to develop long-term strategies for working with a particular set of team members, and the fact that such group work is not graded can send a message that it is not important. Therefore, I divided the students into 24 five-person teams ($N = 120$) for the entire semester. To take advantage of the diversity in the class, I decided to make the groups as heterogeneous as possible. With the assistance of two graduate assistants, I devoted almost five hours of intense effort to the creation of heterogeneous groups on the basis of the grade on the first course Web assignment, departmental major, and class standing. We also looked at the gender composition to be sure that there were no teams in which one woman might be matched with four men and therefore vulnerable to potential sexual harassment. Many students, of course, do not match the stereotypes of their disciplines, but this system makes it statistically more likely that students with different levels of preparation will be working together. We had already asked students to inform us in a confidential e-mail if they had special needs, such as being close to the front or near an aisle, and we placed them in a team that did not rotate with the rest of the class.

Once all of this apparatus had been taken care of, the composition of the teams was posted on the course Web site, and when students arrived in class the second week, an overhead of the seating arrangement told them where their team would be sitting for the first third of the course. I made a point of explaining to the class the reasons for not giving them the freedom to sit wherever they wished, explaining that it was necessary for all of the members of each team to sit together throughout every class. Each day the first member of a team to arrive picked up the group's folder at the back of the classroom and returned it at the end of class, thereby greatly facilitating the distribution of assignments and exercises.

As a group, my students were more open to working in teams than those Professor Schlegel will describe below, but it would be a mistake to assume that everyone in my course understood the value of this work. Therefore, in the first class, I provided ten reasons why I use permanent learning groups, and I made these available on the course Web site (http://www.indiana.edu/~flp). I also made it clear that 15 percent of the final grade would be based on in-class team exercises and that complaints such as "I don't like to work with other people" would be no more relevant in this course than they will be in their future occupations.

There is a good deal of evidence that the teams generated by the process functioned well. A questionnaire distributed at midsemester indicated that the students were generally happy with their teams and that only in only a few cases did a group appear to be nonfunctional. These teams served to give students a chance to practice and to receive feedback both from me and from each other on the essential disciplinary operations of the course. This work was spread over three class periods and interspersed with several minilectures explaining the idea of making assumptions and values explicit. I also led whole-class discussions in which students individually described the basic literal argument, the assumptions, and the values in a passage from an author we were discussing that week, Antonin Artaud. (Examples of this process can be viewed at http://www.indiana.edu/~flp.) I then carefully modeled how I would go about this process in a different passage from Artaud. The teams were then asked to collectively identify the assumptions and values implicit within several other passages, images, and a film.

I had now modeled these basic historical operations and given the students plenty of opportunity to practice these skills and to get feedback. In their teams, they had articulated their understanding of this way of processing cultural artifacts and had heard the ways in which their teammates had internalized this approach. Therefore, it was time to assess whether learning had occurred. I returned to the passage that students had analyzed at the beginning of this process and asked them to repeat what they had done two class periods earlier using the same passage. I then had both sets of answers coded, combined, and randomized. After I graded 120 of these exercises, the two sets of grades were re-sorted, and the average grade for the first attempt was compared with that of the second.

The results were encouraging. There was no appreciable change in the grades assigned to the students' summaries of the literal meaning of the text (an average of 3.11 on the first round and 3.16 on the second). This was to be expected because we had not dealt with this process in the interim between the two assessments. By contrast, the efforts to identify values and assumptions had improved markedly. The average grades on the assumptions increased from 2.7 to 3.4 (an increase of 26 percent), and the identification of values went from 2.5 to 3.2 (an increase of 25 percent). This increase in students' ability to conduct one of the most demanding operations in the course over only three class periods was striking.

Like most assessments of student learning, this process did not produce definitive proof that the combination of systematic modeling and repeated practice of the new operations in the context of learning teams was the sole factor contributing to this result. The results were suggestive, however, and if they are repeated in subsequent semesters, they should provide a strong indication that this approach has validity. There were, of course, a good number of students who did not show improvement across this period and who had still not mastered these ways of analyzing primary materials. In the future, I will work to foster success for even more students. But for now, I have evidence that many students are emerging from my class with new and potentially productive ways of understanding culture that they would not have mastered had I not used learning teams to help decode the disciplines.

Using Teams in Decoding Physiology (Schlegel)

My students are predominantly senior, preprofessional biology majors, all of whom are highly motivated and fiercely competitive; greater than 90 percent go on to study medicine and dentistry and become members of health care or scientific research teams. They are exceptionally good at memorization and solitary study. My students' past success with these learning strategies and their monocular focus on their professional career path represent a bottleneck that significantly interferes with the development of disciplinary thinking.

The central concept of organ system physiology, homeostasis, is described as "the coordinated physiological processes which maintain most of the steady states in the organism" (Cannon, 1929, p. 400). To think like a physiologist, students must learn how to distinguish and employ valid evidence; relate the evidence to physiological process and homeostatic mechanisms; determine the appropriate temporal sequence of events; and learn to seek appropriate resources to inform their thinking, one of the most important resources being each other. Case studies are the focus of each class period, providing students a relevant application of physiological concepts and a means of collaboratively developing their analytical skills (Herreid, 1994).

Because the class is relatively homogeneous, the makeup of teams is less important than in the history course, and students are randomly placed in permanent teams of five at the start of the semester. But a great deal more attention needs to be devoted to overcoming student resistance to and inability to benefit from collaborative learning.

The expectation for my students is that on graduation they will know how to work collaboratively in science and medicine. Yet, few know the names of their peers after four years with one another in various science classrooms and laboratories. At the beginning of the course, many of them express great resistance to working collaboratively, making comments such as, "I am more motivated than my group members," "My group will hinder my ability to get the grade I want in this course," "I have a better science background than my group members," and "I study much better on my own."

Peterson (1997) notes that most students in a problem-based health professions curriculum do not possess the skills necessary to work together to solve problems and are often forced to muddle through a group process in the effort to learn. Research also reveals that even when students are provided the opportunity to learn in groups, the skills and understanding achieved may not be transferable or retained beyond the immediate learning environment (Branch, 2001; Blue, Elam, Fosson, and Bonaminio, 1998; Peterson, 1997). Branch (2001) argues that within medical education, professionalism is not teachable; however, it is learnable. Branch found that providing both active learning and critical reflection improves communication skills and positively influences the development of professional values and attitudes of medical students and subsequently medical professionals. The remainder of this section will focus on principles 10 and 11 (see Exhibit 8.1), assessment of team functioning and learning.

Evaluation of Student Learning and Team Exams. To emphasize the importance of group processes and to keep assessment of students' learning consistent with the methods employed in building disciplinary thinking, teams were used in the exam process. During the semester, there were four objective, case-based exams designed to evaluate students' ability to apply problem-solving skills to organ system physiology. Collaborative learning on exams has been shown to enhance student performance and learning (Rao, Collins, and DiCarlo, 2002) and is consistent with a structured team-learning environment (Schlegel, 2002). Exams were given during a two-hour class period, where students spent the first hour working on their own with no resources and the second hour working on the same exam with their peer group members using their textbook, class notes, and laboratory applications manual. The students' exam score was the sum of their individual and group efforts on twenty-five questions, with a maximum of one hundred points possible.

This assessment method provided an opportunity for students to use the same learning strategies established in the classroom. There has consistently been a 22-percentage point mean increase on exam scores during the semesters when peer groups, rather than individuals, solve the same exam (Figure 8.1). Similarly, performance on semester exams has consistently increased 22 percentage points from the first to the fourth exam.

Student Evaluation of Teamwork. After each of the first two semester exams, students evaluated their group participation. I reviewed their assessment forms and provided feedback to each group; as a whole class, we discussed the evaluation process. Following the third and fourth semester exams, group members assigned a point score that reflected peer participation and

Figure 8.1. Physiology Semester Exams, Fall 2003

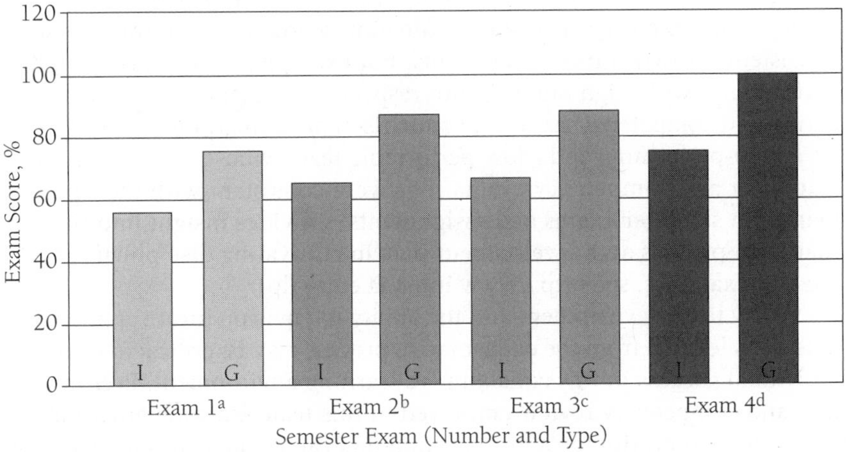

Note: I, individual; G, group
[a]Difference between I and G = 19.5%
[b]Difference between I and G = 22.2%
[c]Difference between I and G = 22.1%
[d]Difference between I and G = 24.6%

contribution to the group effort, which was applied to their semester point total. Allowing students the opportunity for group, self-, and peer evaluation facilitates student understanding of their strengths, weaknesses, inhibitions, and styles of thinking and working (Schlegel, 2002; Michaelson, Bauman Knight, and Fink, 2002). The group exam model coupled with the evaluation process contributed to a 9 percent significant increase on the individual comprehensive final exam over prior semesters with no team learning.

To better understand the student collaborative process and how team learning contributed to development within the discipline, I added two additional assessments: a group history (report and presentation) and a competency evaluation determined for each team member by his or her peers. These assessments were modeled after two aspects of the health care profession, the patient history and the competency-based curricular assessment employed in medical education. The peer competency evaluation was performed before the group history report, and many teams used the language of the competency evaluation in their group history summaries. Many teams developed criteria to guide their team history, and often these criteria incorporated components of the semester group and peer evaluation.

Peer and competency evaluations were consistent with student performance within teams, with two exceptions: a team comprising all men and another all women. Team average evaluation scores and performances were consistent for two-thirds of the teams. For example, teams ranked high in performance were high ranking with respect to the team average peer evaluation and competency scores. A comparison of team group history reports for a high-performing and a low-performing team, whose average scores on team peer and competency evaluations were consistent with their performance on semester exams and assignments, provides insight into the role that team process and development play in cultivating disciplinary thinking (for examples, see http://www.indiana.edu/~flp).

Early team development and the ability to envision future applications of lessons learned from the collaborative process may be critical to team and individual success in this collaborative learning environment. Peer evaluation and competency review employed in this team-learning environment appear to be powerful tools for reflection that can facilitate disciplinary skill development and professional attitudes and behaviors necessary to decode the discipline of physiology for this student population.

References

Blue, A. V., Elam, C., Fosson, S., and Bonaminio, G. "Faculty Members' Expectations of Student Behavior in the Small-Group Setting." *Medical Education Online* [serial online], 1998.

Bosworth, K., and Hamilton, S. J. (eds.). *Collaborative Learning: Underlying Processes and Effective Techniques.* New Directions for Teaching and Learning, no. 59. San Francisco: Jossey-Bass, 1994.

Branch, W. T. "Small-Group Teaching Emphasizing Reflection Can Positively Influence Medical Student's Values." *Academic Medicine,* 2001, 76(12), 1171–1173.

Cannon, W. B. "Organization for Physiological Homeostasis." *Physiological Reviews,* 1929, 9, 399–431.

Cooper, J., and Robinson, S. "Small-Group Instruction in Science, Mathematics, Engineering, and Technology (SMET) Disciplines: A Status Report and an Agenda for the Future." *Journal of College Science Teaching,* 1998, 27(6), 383–388.

Heller, P., Keith, R., and Anderson, S. "Teaching Problem Solving Through Cooperative Grouping. Part 1: Group Versus Individual Problem Solving." *American Journal of Physics Teachers,* 1992, 60, 627–636.

Herreid, C. F. "Case Studies in Science: A Novel Method of Science Education." *Journal of College Science Teaching,* 1994, 23, 221–229.

Johnson, D. W., and Johnson, R. T. *Learning Together and Alone: Cooperative, Competitive, and Individualistic Learning.* 5th ed. Needham, Mass.: Allyn & Bacon, 1999.

Michaelsen, L. K. "Team Learning: A Comprehensive Approach for Harnessing the Power of Small Groups in Higher Education." *To Improve the Academy,* 1992, 11, 107–122.

Michaelson, L. K., Bauman Knight, A., and Fink, L. D. *Team-Based Learning: A Transformative Use of Small Groups in College Teaching.* Westport, Conn.: Greenwood, 2002.

Millis, J. B., and Cottell, P. G. *Cooperative Learning for Higher Education Faculty: Series on Higher Education.* Westport, Conn.: Oryx Press, 1998.

Peterson, M. "Skills to Enhance Problem-Based Learning." *Medical Education Online* [serial online], 1997.

Rao, S. P., Collins, H. L., and DiCarlo, S. E. "Collaborative Testing Enhances Student Learning." *Advances in Physiology Education,* 2002, *26*(1), 37–41.

Schlegel, W. M. "Assessment Is More Than a Collection of Data." *FASEB Journal,* 2002, *16*(5), A756.

Slavin, R. E. *Cooperative Learning: Theory, Research and Practice.* 2nd ed. Needham, Mass.: Allyn & Bacon, 1995.

Springer, L., Stanne, M. E., and Donovan, S. "Measuring the Success of Small-Group Learning in College-Level SMET Teaching: A Meta-Analysis." *Review of Educational Research,* 1999, *69*(1), 21–51.

WHITNEY M. SCHLEGEL is assistant professor of cellular and integrative physiology and director of the undergraduate curriculum at Indiana University School of Medicine. She is also a scholar of the Carnegie Academy for the Scholarship of Teaching and Learning.

DAVID PACE is associate professor of history and codirector of the Faculty Learning Community at Indiana University. He is also a scholar of the Carnegie Academy for the Scholarship of Teaching and Learning.

This chapter outlines the understanding gained when working with faculty to learn about assessment, to develop a plan, and to support them as they carry out and interpret their assessments.

Decoding the Assessment of Student Learning

Lisa Kurz, Trudy W. Banta

While other chapters in this volume present overviews of the Decoding the Disciplines model in its entirety in a variety of disciplinary contexts, this chapter focuses on one step of the model: assessment. This focus reflects assessment's central role in the model and in teaching and learning in general. We also identify the principles of assessment that have been discovered during this program so that instructional consultants or others interested in faculty development can apply them to their own projects. Exhibit 9.1 represents the distillation of these principles.

Because the model is in the form of a circle, the assessment step takes on special importance as both an initiator and an outcome of the process. That is, by demonstrating that students have mastered particular learning tasks that have been defined and modeled in earlier steps, assessment is part of the outcome of the process. But it can also simultaneously be a starting point, providing an impetus for a faculty member to define a bottleneck to students' learning and devise ways of helping students move past that bottleneck.

Despite the importance of assessment, however, it is a step that many faculty might be tempted to skip. One reason for this tendency surely lies in the observation that among faculty in many disciplines, assessment techniques are neither widely understood nor well carried out—understandable consequences of the fact that faculty are experts in their own disciplines, not the discipline of assessing student learning. In fact, many current faculty have had little training in assessment, and what little training they have received has been as apprentices in traditional lecture-test contexts. What makes this assessment even more challenging is that the model encourages

Exhibit 9.1. Encouraging Faculty in Assessment

Preparing Faculty for Assessment

1. Provide information to faculty about the wide variety of assessment strategies.
2. Provide logistical support and encouragement.
3. Be prepared to address various levels of comfort and expertise in using assessment techniques.
4. Help faculty warm up to the idea of doing assessment by engaging them in the use of assessment techniques in their faculty learning community seminars.
5. Show faculty that assessment need not take up much class time and can even be done outside class.
6. Demonstrate to faculty that expertise in assessment is not needed—everyone can find or design assessment techniques that address their needs.
7. Use assessment to help faculty focus on the steps of the Decoding the Disciplines process in addition to subject content.
8. Assist faculty in obtaining Human Subjects Committee approval if they plan to publish their results.

Selecting or Designing Assessment Techniques

9. Determine and define as specifically as possible what students need to learn—that is, what should they know and be able to do to pass through a bottleneck?
10. Determine how students will learn the skills and knowledge identified in no. 9 above.
11. Then select or devise assessment strategies that are as authentic as possible—that is, that enable students to demonstrate that they have mastered the knowledge and skills within the instructional context described in no. 10 above. Assessment strategies must be adapted both to the subject matter or skills and to the types of learning experiences being used.
12. Use both qualitative and quantitative approaches to assessment. (Students' reactions and reflections are at least as helpful in determining the reasons for the success or failure of an instructional innovation as are students' scores on a test or paper.)
13. Use classroom assessments to give students "appropriate and focused feedback early and often" (p. 9).
14. Use assessments to enable faculty "to answer questions they themselves have formulated in response to issues or problems in their own teaching" (p. 9).
15. Be aware that students may need to review and have reinforced the major points of a learning activity before an assessment will reveal changes in their levels of understanding.
16. If results averaged over an entire class do not clearly show improvement, be aware that analysis of trends for individuals may be informative.
17. Be prepared to see only modest increases in student learning on the basis of initial experiments with instructional innovations.

Source: Angelo and Cross, 1993.

the use of active learning techniques and nontraditional ways of teaching. Assessing these teaching techniques often requires strategies that are equally nontraditional and unfamiliar to faculty.

In this chapter, we present an overview of the assessment strategies used by faculty participants in the Indiana University Faculty Learning Community (IUFLC), from the development of assessment plans to the analysis of the resulting data. We write as instructional consultants and advocates for scholarly assessment (Banta, 2002) who have observed the faculty authors of other chapters in this volume as they have experimented with innovations in teaching and learning in their courses and as they selected or designed appropriate assessment techniques. We have also worked with these faculty members to refine and improve their assessment approaches throughout the project. We discuss here the unsuccessful as well as the successful techniques—what did not work as well as what did—and provide some take-home messages on assessment for others who may seek to apply the Decoding the Disciplines model to their own courses. Specific details and example assessments are also available online (http://www.indiana.edu/~flp).

Creating an Assessment Plan

In assessing students' learning, a faculty member must first decide as specifically as possible what subject matter she wants her students to learn (that is, what the focus of the later assessment will be) and how she intends to teach it. These steps, usually the most difficult in creating an assessment plan, are made easier because faculty are taken systematically through the process of answering a series of questions in the first three steps of the model (see nos. 9, 10, and 11 of Exhibit 9.1, "Selecting or Designing Assessment Techniques"). After the faculty participants in the IUFLC completed these initial steps in the FLC two-week seminar, they met individually with the IUFLC codirectors, often accompanied by additional instructional support staff members, to design their assessments.

Although most of the faculty participants were enthusiastic about the prospect of trying out the new active learning techniques they had experimented with in the FLC seminar, their first reaction to the idea of assessing the process was sometimes less positive. At least part of this resistance seemed to be related to notions of assessment as something that is imposed on faculty from above in which they are passive subjects being judged rather than active participants. In addition, the IUFLC experience often presents faculty with the first opportunity of their careers to learn about and practice assessment techniques.

To overcome this resistance, faculty practiced using Classroom Assessment Techniques (CATs; Angelo and Cross, 1993) in the IUFLC seminar. During the IUFLC, faculty fellows designed CATs to assess the results of the "lessons" they presented in the seminar, and the other fellows also suggested assessments they might use. This helped the faculty warm up to the idea of assessment and gave them numerous assessment options. They learned that assessment need not take up much class time and that it can even be done outside of class. They also learned that they need not be experts to use the assessment techniques (such as CATs) that we have found to be particularly successful in the past. However, for faculty to use

CATs or other assessments in their classes, they needed logistical support and encouragement at this stage as well as information or ideas about assessment strategies (see nos. 1 and 2 of Exhibit 9.1, "Preparing Faculty for Assessment").

As consultants designing assessment plans with the faculty participants, we found that it was important for us to strive to understand something about the subject matter that faculty members would be experimenting with and then assessing. It was a challenge to get them to focus on the steps of the model, however, rather than the subject matter of their courses. Part of our job as consultants, then, was to help faculty members take a step back from that content to focus on the larger issues by talking about assessment.

As we moved into discussing the specifics of the assessment plan, part of our function was to point out the different approaches faculty could use (see Table 9.1). Occasionally, we found that effective assessment techniques fell out of the teaching strategies faculty had already devised. In most cases, however, we discussed a variety of specific assessment tools such as CATs (all IUFLC faculty participants were given copies of the 1993 edition of Angelo and Cross). Often we adapted CATs to our purposes and in some cases invented new CATs. Still other possibilities we mentioned involved more traditional assessment data, such as student test scores or grades on papers, although we often suggested reevaluating papers anonymously to remove possible bias. In courses with many sections in which there was a common final exam, the performance of students in the experimental section could be compared with that of students in other sections, either on the exam as a whole or, preferably, on the exam items that focused on the specific material to be assessed. Yet another possibility was comparing the performance of students in the current semester with that of students in previous semesters.

Also on the menu of assessment techniques we brought to the conversation was gathering qualitative information, such as students' reflections and reactions to their learning experiences. Although faculty (particularly those in quantitative disciplines) may not be familiar with the value of this sort of data, we found that it can often provide useful insights into students' thinking as well as their perception of the contribution of the learning experience to their understanding of course content (see, for example, Chapter Seven).

Regardless of the type of assessment a faculty member chose, another important part of our job was to ensure that assessment was specific to both the discipline and the particular cognitive tasks in which the students were engaged. To accomplish this, we asked, "If I were a student, what evidence would show whether I had mastered this step?" Asking this question enabled us to make the assessments authentic and improved our chances of obtaining accurate and valid information about students' mastery.

After the faculty members had chosen assessments, we provided them with logistical support, importantly including assistance in obtaining the

Table 9.1. Types of Assessment Used in Decoding the Disciplines

Type of CAT Used[a]	Where Described, by Chapter, Section
Focused listing	4, Durisen; 5, Gutjahr
Minute paper	5, Ardizzone; 7, Rubin
Defining features matrix	5, Breithaupt
Muddiest point	3, Innes
Conceptest	3, Strome
Background knowledge probe	4, Durisen; 7, Krishnan
Documented problem solution	4, Durisen; 7, Krishnan
One-sentence summary	4, Durisen
Concept map	4, Durisen
Class model	3, Innes; 4, Pilachowski
Storyboard[b]	3, Innes

Type of Assessment Used[c]	Where Described, by Chapter, Section
Some form of pre versus post comparison, often of responses to a CAT or a multiple-choice quiz	3, Zolan; 4, Durisen and Pilachowski; 5, Gutjahr and Breithaupt; 6, Shopkow and Pace; 7, Rubin; 8, Pace and Schlegel
Polling of students	3, Strome
Self-evaluation of group work	8, Schlegel
Exam performance	3, Strome and Zolan; 8, Schlegel
Survey of attitudes	7, Rubin
Rubric for use by students, faculty, or both in grading an essay or paragraph	6, Grim and Pace
Tally of number of pieces of evidence included in students' papers	6, Shopkow
Worksheet	4, Pilachowski; 7, Krishnan
Pyramid exam technique[d]	8, Schlegel
Comparison with students in other concurrent sections or previous sections	8, Schlegel

Note: Total participation: fourteen professors, fourteen courses.
[a]Used by eight professors.
[b]Invented by one of the IUFLC professors.
[c]Used by twelve professors.
[d]Cohen and Henle, 1995.

required permissions for the assessment from the campus Human Subjects Committee (see no. 8 of Exhibit 9.1). Some of the faculty participants had experience with the requirements for the use of human subjects, but many others did not. We wanted to ensure that a lack of familiarity with this process would not prevent faculty from participating in the program. All the IUFLC faculty completed a test certifying that they were familiar with regulations regarding the use of human subjects, and all obtained informed consent from students in their courses for the use of their data in these reports.

Carrying Out the Assessment Plans

To increase the chances of capturing some positive outcomes, we asked all participating faculty to conduct at least two assessments of students' mastery of the learning tasks defined in their bottlenecks. Most did so; one faculty member used only a single assessment, and another used six different assessments (see Table 9.1 for a complete listing of the types of assessments used in this project).

The variability in the types and numbers of these assessments reflected the faculty participants' differing comfort levels and familiarity with assessment techniques. One faculty member, for example, collected a substantial amount of data, both quantitative and qualitative, on her students' group work. Her students wrote a history and analysis of their group's performance and evaluated one another's contributions to the group. In addition, she used a pyramid exam technique (in which students take an exam individually and then immediately take the same exam again working in groups [Cohen and Henle, 1995]) and compared students' individual scores on exams with their group scores. She also used an adapted CAT, the "documented problem solution," at the beginning and end of the semester. For her, our support took the form of helping her decide what data would be most useful from all she had collected. Another faculty member was comfortable only with the "minute paper" CAT. However, he found this information useful and has continued to use it frequently, perhaps because it matches the hands-off attitude of his discipline and encourages his students to take risks in class.

For some of the participating faculty, collecting quantitative data was a familiar part of their disciplines. For example, it was easier for a faculty member in statistics than for one in the humanities to analyze quantitative assessment data, although the professors who used new inquiry modes were often pleased with the explanatory power of these methods.

Most of the faculty chose a CAT (Angelo and Cross, 1993) as their primary assessment tool (see Table 9.1). Among the most popular were "focused listings," "minute papers," "background knowledge probes," "documented problem solutions," and "class models." Another popular CAT was the "Conceptest" developed by Ellis, Landis, and Meeker (n.d.), which has been used widely by IUFLC faculty in addition to the uses reported in this volume. Several of the faculty chose to use a particular CAT twice, before and after a particular learning experience took place. This strategy provided the faculty member with information from each CAT individually and also permitted a pre/postcomparison. Other faculty chose a pair of CATs and administered them sequentially. We found that the CATs that faculty chose almost always required some adaptation to the specific circumstances of the course.

One faculty member (see Chapter Three) invented a new CAT, which we call the "storyboard" CAT. He used the "class model" first, in which the students in his class modeled the steps of a biological process by acting as the chemical components of that process. Then, to give his students more practice in modeling and to consolidate their understanding of the process, he then asked them to illustrate the steps of the recently modeled process in a cartoon or storyboard, similar to those they might see in the textbook. Students also provided a user key and brief explanation of their storyboard panels. Using the new CAT, this professor could determine whether his students were able to translate the three-dimensional process they had modeled in class into a static two-dimensional representation. Using this CAT, the students might also arrive at a better understanding of the two-dimensional representations of other processes in their texts and elsewhere.

We found CATs to be particularly useful forms of assessment for many of the participating faculty because the assumptions underlying them match the assumptions of the Decoding the Disciplines model. For example, Angelo and Cross state that "to improve their learning, students need to receive appropriate and focused feedback early and often," and "the type of assessment most likely to improve teaching and learning is that conducted by faculty to answer questions they themselves have formulated in response to issues or problems in their own teaching" (1993, p. 9). CATs are also learner-centered, teacher-directed, formative, and context-specific, making them a particularly appropriate form of assessment for this project.

In addition to CATs, faculty used a variety of other assessment techniques (Table 9.1). For example, several created their own worksheets or surveys (see http://www.indiana.edu/~flp for examples). Others analyzed students' performance on quizzes, homework assignments, or exams. Still others used rubrics to evaluate students' written work. For example, one faculty member gave short writing assignments at regular intervals in her history course. She selected several of these assignments, some from early in the semester and others from later, and devised a simple rubric to score them. The rubric emphasized the analytical and synthetic skills she was trying to foster in her students. She familiarized us with the rubric and gave us some practice in its use with several student papers selected as benchmarks. We then scored the students' papers and tabulated the results to determine if students' writing demonstrated that they had mastered these skills over the course of the semester.

What Worked and What Did Not

The results of most of the assessments were both clear and positive. Among the most successful assessment strategies were the pre/post comparisons. For example, one faculty member obtained particularly clear evidence of students' mastery of the concept of metaphor in language in his comparison of his students' "focused listings" before and after his lecture on this material (see Chapter Five). Another faculty member's comparison of the "minute papers" his students wrote before and after his classroom activity on sampling distributions clearly demonstrated their mastery of this concept (Chapter Seven). Occasionally, if the pre/post measures were not identical or were not comparable in difficulty, the comparison yielded ambiguous results. In general, however, these analyses were effective.

The CATS provided another effective set of assessment tools. Some CATs provided quantitative data while others yielded more qualitative results, but all provided useful data. The results of some CATs also reminded us that assessments are a beginning as well as an end point. For example, one faculty member's experience made clear that students sometimes need the main points of a classroom learning activity to be reviewed and reinforced before a CAT will be able to reveal their increased understanding.

When faculty chose to use exam or quiz performance as an assessment, the results were occasionally less clear, particularly when the exam consisted mainly of multiple-choice items. Some exam data provided clear evidence that students had grasped the concepts faculty were trying to convey, but the results of other multiple-choice assessments yielded smaller effects. In these situations, it was difficult to unequivocally attribute a student's high score on a test to a previous learning experience because many other factors may have contributed to the student's exam performance. It was also difficult to construct test items that were closely tied to the learning tasks to be mastered. In general, the less specific the assessment was, and the less clearly connected it was to prior active learning experience, the more ambiguous the feedback it provided.

By far the most common concern we had in these assessments, however, was the small size of the effects. In a few cases, this issue may be a matter of the small sample sizes involved—that is, although small class sizes provide an advantage when planning and conducting active learning exercises, they can be a disadvantage when looking for large improvement trends in student learning. In general, however, this concern reflects our lack of knowledge about how big an effect size to expect in assessments such as these. There is a dearth of evidence to guide our expectations in this regard, and we are consequently left with our own impression that many of the improvements we found, while clear, were on the small side. It is also possible, however, that our effect sizes are typical for assessments like ours. In view of these concerns, we made no attempt to calculate the statistical significance of any of our effects.

When an assessment did not yield the results we hoped for, we usually looked at the data we gathered in a different way. For example, if the results averaged over an entire class did not show clear improvement in student learning, we examined the data for individual students to see how many improved, stayed the same, or declined. Often by analyzing individual results in this way, we discovered further bottlenecks to students' learning in addition to those originally identified by faculty members. In this case, we could help the faculty member break down the learning tasks into smaller steps or devise other teaching strategies to help students master these tasks. Using this strategy, faculty could see the assessments as providing the impetus for further innovation in their teaching, going back through the Decoding the Disciplines cycle.

Lessons Learned

Although our assessments sometimes revealed smaller improvements than we hoped for, they also demonstrated the power of the Decoding the Disciplines model in breaking through the cognitive impediments to students' learning. Our assessments show that many of the students in these classes met the goals faculty set for them: they gained a clearer understanding of how biologists, historians, astronomers, statisticians, and members of other disciplines think. In addition, the assessments provided students with valuable feedback about their own mastery of the subject matter. Several faculty reported that their students spontaneously expressed gratitude for the feedback provided by the assessments, and others commented that their students clearly felt empowered by these experiences. Some faculty described the moments when their students made breakthroughs, gaining sudden understanding of concepts that were not clear before. These events provided considerable satisfaction for the faculty as well as for the students.

The assessments have produced other positive outcomes as well. In addition to the improvements in students' learning, our faculty participants also experienced some positive outcomes. For example, it was not only students who had moments of enlightenment as they went through this process; some faculty also experienced breakthroughs in their understanding of the cognitive processes underlying their expertise in their disciplines, which enabled them in turn to devise more effective ways of conveying those processes to students. In addition, the analysis of the assessment data was for many faculty an unexpectedly positive experience. Once a faculty member had obtained positive results using a CAT, for example, this experience seemed to provide motivation for the faculty member to continue investigating new ways to teach course content and incorporate active learning strategies. This motivating effect of using CATs has also been documented elsewhere (Angelo, 1991; Steadman, 1998).

We as instructional consultants have also extracted some valuable lessons from this experience (see Exhibit 9.1). We have acquired a new appreciation for the importance of using more than one assessment technique, for example, and we have learned to look for small increments in learning rather than substantial effects. Because there is little evidence in the literature on which we can base our judgments on this subject, however, we hope that other faculty and instructional consultants will also contribute research on this question. We also have a renewed respect for the importance of assessments that are simple and closely tied to the course and its learning experiences. Finally, as we worked with faculty to refine and improve their

approaches to assessment, we came to recognize that the most effective
assessments were those in which the faculty member succeeded in defining
the basic learning tasks in the initial steps of the Decoding the Disciplines
model. The importance of breaking down a bottleneck into small, manageable steps, defining these as precisely as possible in terms of what students
should know and do, cannot be underestimated. When this is accom-
plished, conducting an effective and useful assessment is a relatively
straightforward matter.

References

Angelo, T. A. "Introduction and Overview: From Classroom Assessment to Classroom
    Research." In T. A. Angelo (ed.), *Classroom Research: Early Lessons from Success.* New
    Directions in Teaching and Learning, no. 46. San Francisco: Jossey-Bass, 1991.
Angelo, T. A., and Cross, K. P. *Classroom Assessment Techniques: A Handbook for College
    Teachers.* 2nd ed. San Francisco: Jossey-Bass, 1993.
Banta, T. *Building a Scholarship of Assessment.* San Francisco: Jossey-Bass, 2002.
Cohen, D., and Henle, J. "The Pyramid Exam." *UME Trends,* 1995, 2, 15.
Ellis, A. B., Landis, C. R., and Meeker, K. "Classroom Assessment Techniques Concept
    Tests" [online]. n.d. Madison: University of Wisconsin. http://www.flaguide.org/cat/
    contests/contests1.php. Accessed June 17, 2004.
Steadman, M. "Using Classroom Assessment to Change Both Teaching and Learning."
    In T. A. Angelo (ed.), *Classroom Assessment and Research: An Update on Uses,
    Approaches, and Research Findings.* New Directions in Teaching and Learning, no. 75.
    San Francisco: Jossey-Bass, 1998.

*LISA KURZ is coordinator of research for instructional support services and
director of writing tutorial services at Indiana University Bloomington.*

*TRUDY W. BANTA is professor of higher education and vice chancellor for plan-
ning and institutional improvement at Indiana University–Purdue University
Indianapolis.*

10

This chapter explains how to plan a faculty learning community that engages a disciplinary inquiry of teaching and learning. It concludes with a five-level assessment of the Indiana University Faculty Learning Community.

Facilitating a Faculty Learning Community Using the Decoding the Disciplines Model

Joan Middendorf

To foster a shift toward a student-centered pedagogy at Indiana University (IU), a small group of professors are selected annually to join a Faculty Learning Community (FLC) in which these fellows study the literature on scholarly teaching, practice new methods that clarify ways of thinking that are essential to their particular discipline, and bring ideas back to their departments and disciplines. In this article, I describe how strategies of planned change guided the IUFLC fellows in the study of the Decoding the Disciplines model (see Chapter One) and resulted in fourteen of them publishing the results in this volume (Chapters Two through Eight).

The IUFLC (originally known as the Freshman Learning Project) came about with our realization that faculty regularly work in isolation to teach their ever-larger classes and that despite their valiant efforts, they are less than satisfied with the results. The challenge we faced was how to expose faculty to the extensive body of literature on teaching and take advantage of new approaches to improve student learning in large classes. Adhering to strategies of planned change, we initiated an FLC and a structure we called the Decoding the Disciplines model within which faculty could begin serious inquiry into their teaching and influence the culture of the academy.

This program has been fortunate to be backed by strong institutional support from the Dean of Faculties Office and the College of Arts and Sciences at Indiana University at Bloomington and the Lilly Foundation of Indianapolis. In particular, W. Raymond Smith, associate vice chancellor of academic affairs at Indiana University at Bloomington, has made invaluable contributions to the creation and the sustenance of the IUFLC. The program has also emerged from a collaboration of a tenure-track faculty member (David Pace, professor in the Department of History) and a professional staff member in academic support services (myself) that began as part of the 1996 IU Summer Leadership Institute and has continued to the present. In 2000, the team added a second professional staff member to help build a culture of assessment (Jennifer Meta Robinson). As each cohort of IUFLC fellows has taken ownership of the program, their energy, enthusiasm, and ideas have moved the IUFLC in directions that were unanticipated and made it a much richer experience.

After providing the background of the program, I outline seven principles for facilitating FLCs, using the IUFLC as an example.

Overview of the Program

The IUFLC began by inviting faculty who teach large classes to participate in a seminar. The groups have usually consisted of eight to fourteen fellows, totaling fifty-three faculty from 1998 to 2003 (nineteen full professors, twenty-seven midcareer professors, and seven pretenure or nontenured faculty). When the IUFLC was started in 1998, the term *faculty learning community* was not prevalent; Cox defined it in 2001 as faculty in small groups of eight to twelve who engaged in an active, collaborative program to enhance teaching and learning, with seminars and activities spaced over a year and beyond. It is clear that our program fits this definition.

As I have previously written, the program "rests on the assumption that the process of rethinking approaches to teaching is best done within a community of teachers and is best disseminated within that same community" (Middendorf, 2001, p. 348; 1999, 2000). To create such a community, the fellows take part in a two-week summer seminar, and then each new IUFLC cohort merges with previous fellows to continue to exchange ideas and to serve as advocates for student learning issues at IU and beyond.

There is nothing remedial about participating in the IUFLC. The fellows are among IU's best and brightest faculty members, all dedicated teachers, most of whom sought tenure or promotion for outstanding research. Yet, most of them had only limited connection with the literature on teaching before their participation in the program.

Why would faculty at a research university want to join? Because just as they like to do well in their research, they want to do the best they can in their teaching. Faculty find the IUFLC "intellectually stimulating" and say, "it is easy to become isolated in our teaching. . . . excellence in research is often a joint effort. Why should excellence in teaching be any different?" And they report that these new techniques make a difference to their students, in statements such as "I have irreversibly altered my view of how to teach effectively" and "I realized . . . students should be having the same movie playing [in] their heads . . . [as I had in mine]," according to faculty feedback we have received.

Seven Principles for Facilitating an FLC

In the process of leading the ten IUFLCs, we have developed a strategy for getting outstanding research faculty to decode their disciplinary thinking and make it more accessible to students. In the remainder of this article, I explain our seven principles for facilitating an FLC as implemented in the IUFLC.

Principle 1: Select Faculty Who Are Likely to Be Emulated. The single most important issue in constituting the IUFLCs has been the selection of its members, and we devoted as much time to this as to designing and leading the summer seminar. From the beginning, we were convinced, as Shulman, Cox, and Richlin have recently argued, that an IUFLC will be more effective at bringing about change if it is constituted of members who have "high position power" and "informal influence and power" (2004, p. 43). We might have asked for nominations from chairpersons and deans, but from experience, we knew that the criteria they used for such appointments would not necessarily be ours.

The other obvious alternative was to have an open application process as Cox describes (2001). But this approach, too, had its downside. The faculty who are most likely to write a successful application are those who have read the literature, attended workshops, and are already invested in new approaches to teaching and learning. Not only are these faculty the least in need of such a program, but they also may be less effective as change agents. Such "innovators" often lack credibility with their peers, and thus, their methods are not likely to be emulated. (However, they are important as demonstrators and testers of new methods.) But if the first to adopt new ideas often have less influence on most of their peers, the opinion leaders, who follow soon after, are crucial in the wider acceptance of new teaching practices because of the "informal" influence they have over their colleagues. (Rogers [1995] has written extensively about the empirical findings on the diffusion of innovations.) We therefore made the identification of opinion leaders one of the foundations of the IUFLCs.

Uncovering opinion leadership can be delicate for outsiders to a department because this is not a characteristic that faculty may feel free to discuss. We invested considerable effort in understanding the social networks in departments to identify these opinion leaders. Technically, we were looking for faculty who represented the "customary views" in their department, who were "central" in departmental communication networks, and who were relied on for their "good judgment" (Middendorf, 2000). To avoid using this jargon, we asked several insiders from each targeted department to suggest professors whose views were especially respected at faculty meetings and whose advice was most often sought by colleagues. Eighty-seven percent of faculty we selected were tenured—another of the criteria for selecting IUFLC fellows because the resources invested in the program would offer long-term payoff for IU. This task has become easier over time with the assistance of IUFLC fellows, who could suggest colleagues who met these criteria.

Principle 2: Take Advantage of Cross-Disciplinary Exchanges. One of the benefits of an FLC is the exchanges that occur in cross-disciplinary discussions of teaching. By talking across disciplines, faculty can gain insights into their own disciplinary thinking and that of their students. Building on Tobias's (1992–1993) work on disciplinary differences, we generally select only one person from any department in each IUFLC. Faculty tend to be more open in their discussions of teaching in this environment, and they find the discussions less negative than sometimes occur in their home departments (Middendorf and Pace, 2002).

When faculty explain basic concepts to colleagues outside their discipline, they become sensitized to how difficult it can be for undergraduates to learn the mental operations required in unfamiliar disciplines. For example, when a historian struggled to understand an astronomer's explanation of the detection of planets beyond the sun, they both gained a better understanding of what students find difficult. The fellow who was acting as a "student" experienced what it was like to be a novice learner, and the fellow who was teaching saw the reactions as the "student" struggled to learn. When a fellow professor could not understand an introductory lesson on structural analysis or quantum mechanics, it was difficult for the professor doing the teaching to blame the student. By delving into the basic course concepts from far-flung disciplines, fellows thus began to rethink their teaching from the students' perspective. Faculty across the disciplines, therefore, valued the opportunity to think deeply about one another's fields.

Principle 3: Provide Appropriate Information When Inviting Faculty to Join an IUFLC. In the early years of the IUFLC, faculty were often unaware of the IUFLC's existence (although this is changing as the reputation of the program spreads). When we approached the identified faculty, our first task was to make them aware of the opportunity without overwhelming them with information. We invited them to participate with a brief and positive message in a letter signed by a well-respected administrator, usually a dean.

Once aware of the IUFLC, faculty became curious. They began to ask questions and seek information. Also, they became concerned about how the IUFLC would affect them, such as, "How much time would this take? What would I gain from this? Who else has been in this IUFLC?" If they did not get good information, they were more likely to turn down the invitation. One of the IUFLC directors met with each individual to answer questions and explain the framework and expectations of the IUFLC. After the first year, we could provide a list of existing fellows and encourage invitees to get more information from the veterans. With personal concerns met, faculty typically agreed to join. This pattern of introducing the fellows gradually to new ideas was inspired by research on the "stages of acceptance" (Rogers, 1995; Dormant, 1999), and this model continues to guide our planning for the preseminar and postseminar activities and for implementation of the seminar (Exhibits 10.1 and 10.2).

Exhibit 10.1. Schedule of Activities for the IUFLC

Preseminar
1. Structured individual interview: What kind of thinking does a student have to do
   on this exam or assignment? How do they do that? (This question is repeated
   several times to dig deeply into disciplinary thinking.)
2. Initial meeting or team building: Fellows share with us a time they succeeded in
   helping students learn.
3. Second meeting or team building: Fellows learn about misconceptions and apply
   them to target course.

Two-week seminar where faculty fellows
1. Go through the Decoding the Disciplines model (Chapter One).
2. Complete readings (available at http://www.indiana.edu/flp and written homework
   "WarmUps" (Novak, Patterson, Gavrin, and Christian, 1999, http://
   webphysics.iupui.edu/jitt/jitt.html).
3. Observe a class in a discipline different from their own.
4. View videos of actual classes showing active and collaborative learning.
5. Participate in active and collaborative activities in the seminar.

Follow-up and subsequent years where faculty fellows
1. Continue to meet to support each other.
2. Take steps to spread the ideas they have learned.

Principle 4: Structure Activities. The IUFLC was structured in two
ways: it had a structured curriculum, providing a systematic way for faculty
to examine their teaching, and it was structured to enhance group process.
Our approach stands in contrast to that followed by many FLCs, which are
open-ended, allowing faculty to develop the agenda. Those FLCs begin by
asking faculty what they would like to achieve (Sandell, Wigley, and
Kovalchick, 2004).

Because we had consciously chosen to open the program up to faculty
who were not always well grounded in contemporary ideas about teaching
and learning, we felt that we needed to move beyond an open agenda to
provide a responsive structure in which faculty could explore these issues
in a systematic manner. At the same time, we wanted the fellows to respond
to the specific problems that arose in their courses and to use all of their
impressive reasoning abilities to come up with original and creative
responses to these problems. Over several years and with the assistance of
the fellows themselves, we thus developed the Decoding the Disciplines
framework for the learning community that grew with their input.

This process begins with interviews in which each new fellow is asked
to provide us with a test or writing assignment that is important for success
in his or her class. The first question we ask is, "What kind of thinking does
a student have to do to succeed at this task?" The follow-up question, which
we repeat many times to dig deeply into disciplinary thinking, is, "How does
the student do that?" This is not an easy question to answer. When faculty
are unable to break down their accustomed ways of thinking into small

Exhibit 10.2. Stages of Acceptance

Stage 1. Awareness: Publicize using a brief, positive message that appeals to faculty needs.

Stage 2. Curiosity: Answer questions and inform about program details.

Stage 3. Visualization: Supply examples so that faculty envision a new way of teaching.

Stage 4. Tryout: Instruct faculty in the Decoding the Disciplines model and teaching methods applicable to each specific course.

Stage 5. Use: Apply technical support and rewards.

Source: Adapted from Dormant, Middendorf, and Marker, 1997.

steps, they sometimes revert to a lecture on the content of their course. The interviewers (usually a team of two support staff) have to remain in the students' perspective, trying to figure out concretely what they would have to do to answer or complete the assignment if they themselves were faced with this task. The interview team produces a one-page write-up of this discussion. (These are available at http://www.indiana.edu/~flp.)

In the weeks leading up to the IUFLC two-week seminar, two meetings serve to enhance group formation and model the way the fellows will operate as coinquirers into student learning. In the initial meeting, the fellows share in pairs a time when they succeeded in helping students learn. Their story is used to introduce each person to the whole group. Thus, the group starts with a positive impression of each other, allowing fellows to get used to the idea that they will work in teams a great deal. In the second meeting, we invite an expert on student preconceptions and misconceptions to address the fellows, who discuss how these concepts apply to their target courses.

Lunch is always served at these meetings and during each day of the summer seminar because sharing a meal is one of the ways to enhance group cohesion. IUFLC meetings are built on food and sharing. After the interview and these first two meetings, fellows have a notion of what IUFLC work entails and look forward to focusing on teaching and learning in a concentrated manner during the seminar.

Principle 5: Provide Models and Practice. During the summer seminar, the fellows meet four hours a day for two weeks as they work through the Decoding the Disciplines process and develop new approaches to teaching. They begin by each identifying a bottleneck to learning in their classes, something that a large number of students find difficult to learn. As the two-week seminar unfolds, IUFLC facilitators provide models of each step and fellows try out and discuss each one in small groups (Exhibit 10.3). This is all accompanied by reading about disciplinary thinking, classroom research, and assessment, along with homework ("WarmUps" by Novak, Patterson, Gavrin, and Christian, 1999), discussion, and practice with teaching methods. For some faculty, this is the first extended period in their careers devoted to analyzing teaching.

Exhibit 10.3. Faculty Learn to Decode Their Discipline

Step 1. Bottleneck: Explain your bottleneck to fellows from different disciplines.

Step 2. Expert thinking: Participate in an individual interview about the specific thinking students need to demonstrate on course papers or exams.

Step 3. Modeling: Demonstrate one learning operation until a fellow from a different discipline can state it in his or her own words.

Step 4. Motivate: Construct and act out "lessons" that violate principles of motivation. Reflect on which principles of motivation your students respond to.

Step 5. Practice: Prepare a lesson on your bottleneck and teach it to the FLC.

Step 6. Assess: Design and use assessments for your own and each other's bottleneck lessons.

Step 7. Share: Communicate new ideas to faculty and administrators outside the FLC through public forum.

To facilitate the development of new strategies for helping students overcome bottlenecks, we help the fellows picture new "movies" in their heads—through articles, presentations by other IU faculty, and videos that create dynamic images about what they might try in the classroom. And throughout the two-week seminar, the fellows themselves experience a variety of active learning techniques that most of them have never seen in practice. Examples of methods, such as team learning, are intermingled with specific instructions on how to implement the method. In the second week, each of the fellows prepares a lesson that deals with a common bottleneck in his or her class. They present their lesson to the rest of the fellows and assess how much the "students" learned. The joy of being a student again, taught by a dedicated teacher, gives great energy to the seminar, at the same time that the fellows provide each other with great models of how to teach in innovative ways.

Principle 6: Provide Ongoing Support After the Seminar. The Decoding the Disciplines model structures faculty inquiry into disciplinary teaching methods while allowing them room for creativity. After trying out their lessons in the IUFLC, faculty become reasonably confident in integrating it into their actual courses. However, the things that work well in the supportive IUFLC environment might not work so well in the classroom. Unfortunately, there is evidence that when faculty first try new teaching methods, their course evaluations may suffer (Allen, Wedman, and Folk, 2001). To continue applying new methods after the seminar, faculty need continuing technical support and rewards.

Technical support is important to help faculty avoid falling back into prior ways of teaching. This is particularly important in the area of assessment. During the seminar, fellows are introduced to the idea of Classroom Assessment Techniques (Angelo and Cross, 1993) and other assessment methods. In the year after the summer seminar, each fellow integrates into one of his or her courses a new module designed to help students get past an important bottleneck and creates a systematic assessment of this learning. Support with the creation of this assessment and assistance with data collection and analysis are crucial (Chapter Nine). One-on-one consultations with academic support staff are readily available when faculty need it. Also, the ongoing peer network available through their IUFLC and occasional meetings of the combined cohort continue to be a source of faculty support when questions arise.

Rewards are important, and although all of the IUFLC fellows are paid a stipend, nonmonetary rewards are also highly valued. These might include mention in the local newspaper or academic publication, appointment to prestigious committees, or grant money from local or national sources. Some of the faculty were motivated to publish, moving from being consumers of the Scholarship of Teaching and Learning in the IUFLC to being producers of systematic, scholarly research about teaching and learning in their disciplines. Others find value in being part of a cohort of faculty dedicated to student learning. Belonging to the IUFLC is itself a reward, with its challenge to think in new ways and the sociability among fellows.

Principle 7: Track Effectiveness in Multiple Ways.   Over time we have improved evaluation practices for the IUFLC. We learned that different kinds of data provide different levels of accountability (Patton, 1997), so we now collect five levels of data (see Exhibit 10.4). For example, our main measures were originally inputs and satisfaction surveys. Measures of inputs to the IUFLC, such as how funding is spent, are considered low-accountability data because they are not connected to outcomes attained. That is, does it matter how much we spend on the program if we cannot demonstrate improvements in students' disciplinary thinking skills? After a while, we learned to track changes in faculty behavior and, finally, to assess students' learning of specific skills, which are considered high-accountability data because they provide evidence as to whether desired results are being achieved. We use multiple measures to assess the IUFLC, hoping the evidence justifies support from our administrative sponsor and continued funding (Middendorf, 2001). We present data about resources expended, participation, satisfaction, changes in faculty practice, and, most important, effects on student learning.

Resources Expended

What are the inputs spent on the IUFLC? Annual out-of-pocket costs are $52,000. In addition, 20 percent of one staff member's time is contributed in kind. Current fellows receive a stipend of $2,500. The eleven 2003 fellows will teach an estimated 23,925 students in the next five years, which represents a cost of $2.17 per student to run the IUFLC.

Exhibit 10.4. Effectiveness Measures for an FLC

Evaluation Measure	Question	Indicators	Data Source	Accountability Level
Resources Expended	What inputs are provided to the FLC?	Costs (money spent); staff time; faculty time; no. of students affected; per student costs	Program budget; registrar's office	Low
Participation	What are the participant characteristics?	Faculty rank; disciplines; no. of students taught	Available IU records	Low
Satisfaction	What are faculty reactions to the FLC (positive, negative, and suggestions)?	Participant ratings and comments to be used for formative improvements and as a basis for continued engagement with FLC	Surveys; interviews; and unsolicited emails of FLC participants (see Appendix)	Medium
Changes in Practice	What changes occurred in faculty behaviors over time: 1. in their teaching; 2. in disseminating new ideas about teaching?	Developed or redesigned a course or part of a course; presented about teaching; prepared course portfolio; published about teaching; received outside grant funding for a teaching project; researched teaching (SOTL); advocated for teaching as an administrator or on a committee	Surveys of FLCers; self-reports	Medium-High
Effects on Student Learning	What has been the impact on student learning?	To assess the degree and nature of student learning in the discipline specific learning tasks through the use of materials generated during the run of each course. The materials used are all regularly required elements of the course collected during the 2003–2004 academic year.	Materials generated as a regular part of a course: assignments; classroom assessment techniques; in-class group exercises; exams and papers. Similar measures from previous semesters may be used for comparison, such as average scores on an exam question or entire exams.	High

Participation

What are the characteristics of the participants and their numbers? Fifty-three fellows participated in the large-class IUFLC from 1998 to 2003, going from across the disciplines: humanities (sixteen), social sciences (twelve), sciences (sixteen), and professional schools (nine), with twenty-seven tenured and nineteen faculty promoted to full professor. These faculty have taught classes that enrolled 34,006 students as of spring semester 2003.

Satisfaction

How do faculty react to the IUFLC? (See this chapter's Appendix for the IUFLC survey questions.) We found that fellows are enthusiastic about the IUFLC, with one stating, "This was the most intellectually stimulating two weeks of my fifteen-year career at Indiana University. I am very excited about introducing innovative teaching techniques to my classes." Another fellow related that halfway through a guest lecture for 170 students, "I . . . told them about this movie I was playing in my imagination, asked them to play this movie in their head. . . . They clearly were much more tuned into the lecture and concept I was trying to get across after that." One professor enthused that because he used the principles of the IUFLC, his students were now doing "seminal, ground-breaking, and paradigm-shifting science."

Changes in Practice

What changes occurred in faculty behavior? We surveyed faculty about activities following their participation in the IUFLC to track changes regarding their teaching as well as their dissemination of new ideas about teaching. For teaching, we tallied the development of new courses and the revision of old ones or more subtle reorientations of teaching strategies. For dissemination of ideas, we tallied a multitude of microinitiatives involving one-on-one conversations with colleagues, informal presentations to colleagues, sharing Web sites and teaching modules with colleagues, and more formal efforts such as grants, committee work, conference presentations, and publications. Positive outcomes of the program include:

Two fellows were accepted into the Carnegie Academy for the Scholarship of Teaching and Learning, in part on the basis of the work they began in the IUFLC.
A fellow became a member of the University Classroom Planning Committee and effectively lobbied for classroom spaces more suitable for active and collaborative learning.
The IUFLC program was cited in a *Time* magazine article (Barovick, 2001) ranking Indiana University the Number One College of the Year.

Three fellows received grants for teaching-oriented programs totaling
$3,230,000.

Fellows published one book and fifteen journal articles on teaching issues,
in addition to those included in this volume (nine of the fourteen coau-
thors had never published anything about teaching previous to this volume, and four had published only one article about teaching).

Fellows made more than thirty-five presentations on teaching (twenty-six
local, four state, four national, and one international).

The Decoding the Disciplines model appears to be effective in hasten-
ing the spread of innovative teaching approaches. The IUFLC has united
the efforts of faculty in a number of fields and provided a method for pur-
suing the Scholarship of Teaching and Learning. After the IUFLC experience, a number of faculty have gone on to positions of formal influence and
power, such as administrative posts and campus and national committees.
Now, armed with the knowledge of scholarly teaching, they are ready and
able to become advocates for teaching and learning issues.

Effects on Student Learning

What has been the effect on student learning? With the Decoding the
Disciplines process, we can now get a clearer idea of which disciplinary
ideas students do or do not comprehend. Equipped for the first time with
precise assessment tools beyond student evaluations of teaching, faculty
have begun collecting quantitative and qualitative data on the effectiveness
of their teaching strategies.

These and other indicators have convinced university administrators
that the IUFLC has been well worth the time and money they have invested.
We have only begun to experience the beneficial effects of this ever-
increasing community of teacher-scholars, and there is every reason to
believe that the learning of future generations of students will be greatly
increased by this program and by the commitment of its fellows to find new
ways to teach the thinking of their disciplines.

Appendix

2004 Faculty Learning Community Confidential Seminar Evaluation
1. In each of the categories below, what did you think were the best:
   • Readings?
   • People / Presenters?
   • Activities?
2. We are constantly changing the FLC seminar.
   • What are the one or two elements of the program that you would least like to
     see us drop in the future?
   • What do you think could most easily be dispensed with?
3. What activities do you foresee engaging in as a result of your participation
in FLC? Please indicate high, medium, or low chance of engaging in each of these
activities.

- Presentation/s about teaching?

High   Medium   Low

- Course portfolios?

High   Medium   Low

- Develop or redesign a course or part of a course (besides the one you developed for FLP)?

High   Medium   Low

- Publications about teaching?

High   Medium   Low

- Receive outside grant funding for a teaching project?

High   Medium   Low

- Research projects on teaching (SOTL)?

High   Medium   Low

- Administrative or committee service where you advocate for teaching?

High   Medium   Low

4. In what ways do you expect the FLC experiences to change what you do in your class(es)?

5. When (which part of the semester) will you teach your model lesson?

6. How useful/valuable did you find the FLC seminar?

Worthless   1   2   3   4   Very Valuable

7. If next year a colleague said he or she has been asked to join the FLC, what would you say to them?

References

Allen, G. K., Wedman, J. F., and Folk, L. C. "Looking Beyond the Valley: A Five-Year Case Study of Course Innovation." *Innovative Higher Education,* 2001, *26*(2), 103–119.

Angelo, T. A., and Cross, K. P. *Classroom Assessment Techniques: A Handbook for College Teachers.* 2nd ed. San Francisco: Jossey-Bass, 1993.

Barovick, H. "Indiana University: A Web of Friendly Interest Groups Makes This Big Research Institution Feel Less Intimidating." *Time,* Sept. 10, 2001, 66–67.

Cox, M. D. "Faculty Learning Communities: Change Agents for Transforming Institutions into Learning Organizations." *To Improve the Academy,* 2001, *19,* 69–93.

Dormant, D. "Implementing Human Performance Technology in Organizations." In H. Stolovitch and E. Keeps (eds.), *Handbook of Human Performance Technology.* San Francisco: Jossey-Bass, 1999, pp. 237–259.

Dormant, D., Middendorf, J. K., and Marker, A. W. *Change Mapping^SM Participant Guide.* Bloomington, Ind.: Dormant, 1997.

Middendorf, J. "A Case Study in Getting Faculty to Change." *To Improve the Academy,* 1999, *17,* 203–224.

Middendorf, J. "Finding Key Faculty to Influence Change." *To Improve the Academy,* 2000, *18,* 83–93.

Middendorf, J. "Getting Administrative Support for Your Project." *To Improve the Academy,* 2001, *19,* 346–359.

Middendorf, J., and Pace, D. "Overcoming Cultural Obstacles to New Ways of Teaching: The Lilly Freshman Learning Project at Indiana University." *To Improve the Academy,* 2002, *20,* 208–224.

Novak, G. M., Patterson, E. T., Gavrin, A. D., and Christian, W. *Just-in-Time Teaching: Blending Active Learning with Web Technology.* Upper Saddle River, N.J.: Prentice Hall, 2004. (Sample materials available at http://www.jitt.org)

Patton, M. Q. *Utilization-Focused Evaluation: The New Century Text.* Thousand Oaks, Calif.: Sage, 1997.

Rogers, E. M. *Diffusion of Innovations.* 4th ed. New York: Free Press, 1995.

Sandell, K. L., Wigley, K., and Kovalchick, A. "Developing Facilitators for Faculty Learning Communities." In M. D. Cox and L. Richlin (eds.), *Building Faculty Learning Communities*. New Directions for Teaching and Learning, no. 97. San Francisco: Jossey-Bass, 2004, pp. 51–62.

Shulman, G. M., Cox, M. D., and Richlin, L. "Institutional Considerations in Developing a Faculty Learning Community Program." In M. D. Cox and L. Richlin (eds.), *Building Faculty Learning Communities*. New Directions for Teaching and Learning, no. 97. San Francisco: Jossey-Bass, 2004, pp. 41–49.

Tobias, S. "Disciplinary Cultures and General Education: What Can We Learn from Our Learners?" *Teaching Excellence*, 1992–1993, 4(6), 1–3.

JOAN MIDDENDORF *is codirector of the Faculty Learning Community at Campus Instructional Consulting, Indiana University.*

11

This chapter presents a vision in which the kinds of thinking and learning that are commonly required of students become a regular part of the teaching and scholarship within every discipline.

Future of Decoding the Disciplines

Joan Middendorf, David Pace

Our experience with Decoding the Disciplines has been so encouraging that we are beginning to be able to imagine where it might lead. Instead of the generic teaching guidelines such as "encourage student interaction" that many faculty encounter, it is possible to imagine discipline-specific maps for student learning in which Decoding the Disciplines

- Helps faculty focus on students' thinking skills, rather than exclusively on content
- Encourages faculty to understand why many students have difficulty in their discipline
- Brings assessment into the mainstream of faculty practice and helps make the collection of data a normal component in a faculty career
- Offers real evidence for faculty decisions about where to focus attention and make changes
- Provides a yardstick that will allow faculty to more precisely evaluate gains in student learning
- Makes faculty in different disciplines better able to share insights into operations that make parallel demands across disciplines—for example, methods to help students visualize in disciplines as far-flung as nano-chemistry and astronomy

But when we really dream, we envision the effects that Decoding the Disciplines might have on university teaching, working in concert with other vitally important approaches to the scholarship of teaching and learning. And we imagine an academy in which there exists within each discipline a literature that defines the kinds of thinking that are commonly required of students; in which learning the nature of disciplinary expectations is a part of preparing future faculty in every graduate program; in which faculty will cease reinventing the basic "wheels" of teaching in their field, and the achievements of one insightful teacher will become the property of all members of the discipline; in which the distance between being a teacher and being a scholar of teaching and learning will begin to disappear; and in which the intellectual powers of the professoriate are brought to bear fully on the challenges of helping students learn.

JOAN MIDDENDORF is codirector of the Faculty Learning Community at Campus Instructional Consulting, Indiana University.

DAVID PACE is associate professor of history and codirector of the Faculty Learning Community at Indiana University at Bloomington. He is also a fellow of the Carnegie Academy for the Scholarship of Teaching and Learning.

INDEX

111

Back Issue/Subscription Order Form

Copy or detach and send to:
Jossey Bass, A Wiley Imprint, 989 Market Street, San Francisco CA 94103 1741

Call or fax toll free: Phone 888 378 2537 6:30AM – 3PM PST; Fax 888 481 2665

Back Issues: Please send me the following issues at $27 each
(Important: please include ISBN number with your order.)

_____

_____

_____

$ _____   Total for single issues

$ _____   SHIPPING CHARGES: SURFACE   Domestic Canadian

First Item	$5.00	$6.00
Each Add'l Item	$3.00	$1.50

For next day and second day delivery rates, call the number listed above.

Subscriptions   Please __ start __ renew my subscription to *New Directions for Teaching and Learning* for the year 2___ at the following rate:

U.S.	__ Individual $80	__ Institutional $170
Canada	__ Individual $80	__ Institutional $210
All Others	__ Individual $104	__ Institutional $244
Online Subscription		__ Institutional $170

**For more information about online subscriptions visit
www.interscience.wiley.com**

$ _____   Total single issues and subscriptions (Add appropriate sales tax for your state for single issue orders. No sales tax for U.S. subscriptions. Canadian residents, add GST for subscriptions and single issues.)

__Payment enclosed (U.S. check or money order only)
__VISA __ MC __ AmEx #_____ Exp. Date _____

Signature _____ Day Phone _____
__ Bill Me (U.S. institutional orders only. Purchase order required.)

Purchase order # _____
                Federal Tax ID13559302   **GST 89102 8052**

Name _____

Address _____

_____

Phone _____ E mail _____

For more information about Jossey Bass, visit our Web site at www.josseybass.com

TL93   **Valuing and Supporting Undergraduate Research**
        Joyce Kinkead
        The authors gathered in this volume share a deep belief in the value of
        undergraduate research. Research helps students develop skills in problem
        solving, critical thinking, and communication, and undergraduate
        researchers' work can contribute to an institution's quest to further
        knowledge and help meet societal challenges. Chapters provide an overview
        of undergraduate research, explore programs at different types of
        institutions, and offer suggestions on how faculty members can find ways to
        work with undergraduate researchers.
        ISBN: 0-7879-6907-9

TL92   **The Importance of Physical Space in Creating Supportive Learning
        Environments**
        Nancy Van Note Chism, Deborah J. Bickford
        The lack of extensive dialogue on the importance of learning spaces in
        higher education environments prompted the essays in this volume. Chapter
        authors look at the topic of learning spaces from a variety of perspectives,
        elaborating on the relationship between physical space and learning, arguing
        for an expanded notion of the concept of learning spaces and furnishings,
        talking about the context within which decision making for learning spaces
        takes place, and discussing promising approaches to the renovation of old
        learning spaces and the construction of new ones.
        ISBN: 0-7879-6344-5

TL91   **Assessment Strategies for the On-Line Class: From Theory to Practice**
        Rebecca S. Anderson, John F. Bauer, Bruce W. Speck
        Addresses the kinds of questions that instructors need to ask themselves as
        they begin to move at least part of their students' work to an on-line format.
        Presents an initial overview of the need for evaluating students' on-line work
        with the same care that instructors give to the work in hard-copy format.
        Helps guide instructors who are considering using on-line learning in
        conjunction with their regular classes, as well as those interested in going
        totally on-line.
        ISBN: 0-7879-6343-7

TL90   **Scholarship in the Postmodern Era: New Venues, New Values, New
        Visions**
        Kenneth J. Zahorski
        A little over a decade ago, Ernest Boyer's *Scholarship Reconsidered* burst upon
        the academic scene, igniting a robust national conversation that maintains
        its vitality to this day. This volume aims at advancing that important
        conversation. Its first section focuses on the new settings and circumstances
        in which the act of scholarship is being played out; its second identifies and
        explores the fresh set of values currently informing today's scholarly
        practices; and its third looks to the future of scholarship, identifying trends,
        causative factors, and potentialities that promise to shape scholars and their
        scholarship in the new millennium.
        ISBN: 0-7879-6293-7

TL83   **Evaluating Teaching in Higher Education: A Vision for the Future**
Katherine E. Ryan
Analyzes the strengths and weaknesses of current approaches to evaluating
teaching and recommends practical strategies for improving current
evaluation methods and developing new ones. Provides an overview of new
techniques such as peer evaluations, portfolios, and student ratings of
instructors and technologies.
ISBN: 0-7879-5448-9

TL82   **Teaching to Promote Intellectual and Personal Maturity: Incorporating
Students' Worldviews and Identities into the Learning Process**
Marcia B. Baxter Magolda
Explores cognitive and emotional dimensions that influence how individuals
learn, and describes teaching practices for building on these to help students
develop intellectually and personally. Examines how students' unique
understanding of their individual experience, themselves, and the ways
knowledge is constructed can mediate learning.
ISBN: 0-7879-5446-2

NEW DIRECTIONS FOR TEACHING AND LEARNING IS NOW AVAILABLE ONLINE AT WILEY INTERSCIENCE

What is Wiley InterScience?

Wiley InterScience is the dynamic online content service from John Wiley & Sons delivering the full text of over 300 leading scientific, technical, medical, and professional journals, plus major reference works, the acclaimed Current Protocols laboratory manuals, and even the full text of select Wiley print books online.

What are some special features of Wiley InterScience?

Wiley Interscience Alerts is a service that delivers table of contents via e mail for any journal available on Wiley InterScience as soon as a new issue is published online.
EarlyView is Wiley's exclusive service presenting individual articles online as soon as they are ready, even before the release of the compiled print issue. These articles are complete, peer reviewed, and citable.
CrossRef is the innovative multi publisher reference linking system enabling readers to move seamlessly from a reference in a journal article to the cited publication, typically located on a different server and published by a different publisher.

How can I access Wiley InterScience?

Visit http://www.interscience.wiley.com.

Guest Users can browse Wiley InterScience for unrestricted access to journal tables of contents and article abstracts, or use the powerful search engine.
Registered Users are provided with a *Personal Home Page* to store and manage customized alerts, searches, and links to favorite journals and articles. Additionally, Registered Users can view free online sample issues and preview selected material from major reference works.
Licensed Customers are entitled to access full text journal articles in PDF, with select journals also offering full text HTML.

How do I become an Authorized User?

Authorized Users are individuals authorized by a paying Customer to have access to the journals in Wiley InterScience. For example, a university that subscribes to Wiley journals is considered to be the Customer.
Faculty, staff and students authorized by the university to have access to those journals in Wiley InterScience are Authorized Users. Users should contact their library for information on which Wiley journals they have access to in Wiley InterScience.

ASK YOUR INSTITUTION ABOUT WILEY INTERSCIENCE TODAY!